JLGERHARDT

Godscout

.COM

WANT TO SEE GOD? LOOK.

Swallowed Up: A Story about How My Brother Died. And I Didn't.

Paperback ISBN: 9781731019226

JL GERHARDT

SWALLOWED UP

A story about how my brother died.
And I didn't.

To Jeff, for being brave and faithful to God's call. Your obedient words stirred me to my own brave, faithful obedience.

To Mom and Dad, for grieving with hope, courage, vulnerability, and wisdom.

To Justin, for partnering in pain and partnering in joy.

And to London and Eve, for laughter like strung lights.

CONTENTS

FOREWORD

Bobby Mays was my best friend. My wife's brother. My comrade. And then, when I was 23 years old, I preached his funeral.

I shed a lot of tears reading what my wife has written here. It opened old wounds, jostled pain that's always simmering somewhere below the surface. More than that, though, I found myself asking as I read, *How is it that there's light on every page??*

Here, I'm convinced, is why:

It's because she is awake to the glimmer of an enchanted world. This is a story about what it means to stumble through a fallen, but Inhabited, place. The wires are live—charged with danger and potential. The soil is restless—teeming with creatures that might inspire wonder or inject venom, or both. The veil is thin in this world of Gerhardt's—and she invites us to consider that her world is not different than ours: awash with sorrow and joy, fear and hope, absence and Presence.

I can promise you this: you will find yourself in this story. As you encounter death on these pages, you will laugh and you will cry and you will—strange as it may seem—feel very much alive.

If you're shuffling through the wilderness of grief, thirsty for a cloud by day and fire by night, may God use this book to guide you.

-Justin Gerhardt

Must not all things at the last be swallowed up in death?

Plato

Therefore we do not lose heart... For our light and momentary troubles are achieving for us an eternal glory that far outweighs them all. So we fix our eyes not on what is seen, but on what is unseen, since what is seen is temporary, but what is unseen is eternal. For we know that if the earthly tent we live in is destroyed, we have a building from God, an eternal house in heaven, not built by human hands...so that what is mortal may be swallowed up by life.

2 Corinthians 4:16–5:4

PART ONE

Surge

noun:

a sudden powerful forward or upward movement, especially by a crowd or by a natural force such as the waves or tide

CHAPTER 1

A COMMON GRIEF

"Death has climbed in through our windows."

Jeremiah 9:21

This story starts with a phone call too early in the morning. I'm still asleep when the phone rings. It's a landline cordless phone with a built-in message machine, because this is 2002 and though we have cell phones people still don't call you on them much, especially not when the call is like this call, the kind of call for which you should be tethered to something, something solid and unlikely to buckle, like the wall of this brick house, like the land.

The phone rings and I reach for it. I don't remember reaching for it. I push it my husband's way. He's the preacher, the one who gets calls at 6 a.m. on Saturday mornings. The sun, already up, bounces around the room, alighting on the white sheets and blanket, so maybe it's not 6. 7? He listens while I drop back to sleep. He says, "Okay. We'll pray," and hangs up.

I rub my eyes. I'll wake to pray.

For Margaret down the street who has cancer? For those folks on the farm whose son keeps running away? Some family at church with some can't-wait need?

"Jen, that was your Papa," he says, and the cast list of faces needing prayers is rewritten. We're praying for *us.*

I'd tell you how my husband Justin's face looked when he told me what he's about to tell me, but I don't remember. All I remember are the white sheets and the sunlight and the way my whole body crumples into the folds of fabric when he speaks.

He says, "Bobby didn't make it home last night."

Your brother, who was driving home from college, who called here last night, who you just saw the other day, who helped you install your mailbox in that hard Alabama clay, who was driving that road we've driven a dozen times now from Tennessee to home, who played Play-Doh Barber Shop with you in the backyard when you were six, who skipped school with you on perfect 80-degree days when you were sixteen—your brother didn't make it home last night.

He should have made it home. He should have made it home hours ago.

There's something we aren't saying. "We" being Papa or my mom, who talked to Papa—her dad—on the phone because she didn't want to call me herself. "We" being Justin and me on this bed in this room alone. All "we" are saying is that Mom waited up all night, that she took calls every hour to help keep him awake, but the calls stopped coming. And he stopped answering her calls. And his car wasn't in the driveway, and his body wasn't in his bed.

Justin says "we're" calling the police. Maybe Bobby's in a ditch somewhere and needs help. Maybe his car broke down and his phone ran out of power.

"We're" saying he's missing, but I know we know he's gone.

When I was little, my Papa asked me to pray because we ran out of gas in the middle of the woods in Appalachia on vacation. We hadn't seen a car in an hour, but I prayed, and as soon as I said "amen," a car pulled up with help. At the beach one time my mom asked me to pray about the weather; I don't know why she asked, but I prayed, and when I did it seemed like the skies shifted, like the clouds received orders from higher up to turn back. Mom and Papa and my dad and my uncles, they all asked me to pray when what we were asking seemed too much. This morning I am being called in to throw the Hail Mary pass.

I pray with all the confidence in the world, out loud, holding my husband's hand, "God, You raised Mary and Martha's brother from the dead. You love me just as much as You loved them. Raise my brother, too."

And the phone rings and it's Papa and he says, "Jennifer, Bobby's dead."

My grief isn't special.

I lost a brother, a brother I loved very much, in a tragic and surprising car accident. He was sober. He was a great kid. Everybody loved him. He loved God. The grieving might have been harder if he'd been a jerk who'd died drunk. Harder still if he'd hit another person. But no, he was wonderful, and I wish he'd lived to meet my daughters and throw them in the air. My loss is not more in heft or height than other kinds of loss. Sometimes it seems small by comparison.

My friend Kim's brother died in a car accident, too. A semi hit him head-on. Her brother, her sister-in-law, and her two nieces all died. Her nephew lived and now he lives in her house, him and all his pain and angst and grief and teenage hormones. Kim's grief seems more impressive to me, but she promises me it's not so bad. *You could handle it*, she says.

My mom was 24 when she lost her mom to cancer. 40 when her son died. 51 when her dad died. She told me, *When both your parents are dead, it's like you don't have anywhere to go. Like you don't have a home.* That seems like a lot to carry.

My dad's sister died at 41. Her partner found her dead in the bed in the morning. Some kind of heart something, or blood clot. Nobody knew she was sick. She died a year and a half after my brother. My dad's dad died of complications due to a surgery we thought was successful. He died in his chair, taking a nap. Dad's dad died two weeks after mom's dad died. I told my Nana I was writing a book about death, and she said, "Well, we've certainly had enough experience with it."

My friend Brittany's husband died in a car accident. They'd been married for just short of four years. My friend Laura's husband died cutting down a tree. They'd been married for five years and had a baby. The young widow seems like the saddest kind of mourner, but some people say, "At least they can start over." *I don't know about that.*

My friends Joy and Stephen lost their first baby just days after she was born. They took pictures in the hospital of her last moments of life. Is that kind of grief, parents burying a baby, all promise and hope and no memories—is that the hardest kind of grief?

I'm not writing this book about grief, about mourning my brother, because I have a corner on grief, because I've experienced it more fully or known it to some extraordinary degree. I'm writing about my experience exactly because it's not special. I'm writing this book because maybe what I went through is like what you went through when you lost your brother or sister or friend or parent or spouse or teacher or child.

How we react in the rubble of death is, of course, personal and unique, but it's also mostly built from the same basic blocks. Most mourners get angry. We're all sad. Everyone I've talked to feels that thing in their gut like there's a scrunched up plastic bag in there, or that weight on their shoulders like they're carrying a backpack full of bricks. Most of us feel at least some bit of regret or guilt. We're all tired, every one of us. No matter who you've lost, you can relate to someone else who's lost someone, too.

I'm writing this story because it's common, and because its being common doesn't make it any less hard. For me or for you.

My brother died fifteen years ago. He was 20. I was 21. He hit a tree with his car when he fell asleep and drifted off the highway in the rain with his cruise control on. People saw it happen. They said he never hit his brakes. The coroner said he didn't think Bobby woke up, that he just hit the tree in his sleep and died instantly. Maybe the coroner told us that because the scene was so gruesome, because the car was crumpled like paper, because my brother's face was so smashed the funeral home people couldn't reconstruct it to look like him and we had to close the casket and I never got a chance to see him one last time. I didn't need to see his face. His hands would have been enough. But no.

His wreck had been an hour or so away from our home in Florida. He'd almost made it—a sixteen-hour trip from Nashville to Clearwater. My dad drove to collect his stuff, so much stuff, every single thing he owned packed into the back of his SUV. He was coming home from college for good, to live at home and finish up locally. Cheaper, more practical. While dad did the quiet, painful work of bringing Bobby home, the parts of him he could gather into trash bags and stuff in the back of his car, Mom stayed still and welcomed the gathering mourners bringing food and hugs, awkward words and paper plates—so we didn't have to do dishes. She took phone calls, so many phone calls, and figured out where everyone would stay.

She also called me every hour to make sure I was still alive.

It's strange how much the bereaved are called upon to do in the moments after finding out their person is dead. My jobs included calling Bobby's best friend from college to tell him the news (which sucked exactly as much as you think it might), booking an immediate flight home to Florida (via my grandfather who was paying but was also bad at talking to airlines over the phone or using the computer to book flights), packing for a trip that might last a month (with no clean clothes in the house), and answering the door when, while on the phone with Bobby's friend, I heard the doorbell ring and friends of mine showed up excited because they'd decided to buy the house right beside us. Their smiles collapsed at the sight of our tear-wrecked faces.

That was the first time I saw someone's face change when they heard the news, the first time I watched a person, hit by a crashing, unexpected wave, lose her bearings and struggle for something to say, some rope to hold onto. It would happen a hundred more times. It still happens today.

Just a couple weeks ago, I was working at the church building, pulling weeds with a new friend, and he made a joke about my brother because he'd heard Justin tell a story about

Bobby, a funny story about how they'd taken the T tops off his 280Z while driving and it hadn't gone so well. This new friend made a joke about the brother he thought was alive, and I wanted so much just to pretend he was still alive so I didn't have to tell him and watch his face fall.

Sometimes I feel like I'm walking around with a grenade.

So, do you have any brothers or sisters?

Older or younger?

Where does he live?

Do I say heaven? My dead brother living in Heaven ruins small talk.

When my friends and new neighbors left, I packed my dirty clothes into my suitcase. I tried to pack, anyway. Mostly I sat in my closet crying, trying to imagine a world in which I was picking out a dress for my 20-year-old brother's funeral. My husband found me there, picked me up, and held me until I'd recovered enough to forget what was happening and finish the tasks and get in the car and drive to the airport.

On our way, I said, "Let's stop at Chick-fil-A for lunch. Bobby loved Chick-fil-A," and it was the first time I'd talked about him in the past tense. So I wept in the drive-thru line. And when Justin handed me the sandwich I felt ridiculous, ridiculous for wanting a sandwich to help me feel close to my brother, and I threw my sandwich out the window.

I wasn't hungry.

Our flight took off on time. I sat beside my husband and held his hand and cried. I can't measure how much I cried in those first 24 hours. It was like Bobby's dying (something that still wasn't real, even if it had immediately changed every single thing) broke a water main inside me. Everything in me burst out of me—light, love, hope. Anger, pain, confusion. Every ounce of energy and clarity. I wept and moaned when the woman who worked for Delta in Atlanta said our connecting flight was canceled. I cried on the floor of the airport waiting for a storm to pass. I cried in the bathroom. I cried in the second plane. I cried when my in-laws picked us up at an airport an hour away from our town because it was the only one we could fly into during the storm. I cried when they saw me crying and couldn't look in my eyes. I cried in the back of the car while Justin filled them in on the details of what had happened. I cried when I pulled into my parents' driveway and walked up to the house and saw my mom on the couch through the glass door, knowing I was not the child she'd been expecting, not the one she most wanted to see. I cried when she hugged me. I cried when I hugged my dad. I cried in my brother's bed, the only place to sleep because my parents had turned my room into an office. The flood of me-filled tears rose, tears drowning me and drowning those who came close enough to try and rescue me. In a few days, when the water didn't gush so much, I'd realize I'd run out of me to leak. I was empty, emptied.

We said grief is common. It is because death is common. Everyone does it, dying, and the shrapnel of it hits everyone close. To be a slowly or not-so-slowly dying human in relationship with other dying humans is to be a mourner. We are all the bereaved.

The first person who dies in the Bible is not one of the first people. He's the fourth. When he dies, he's the youngest person on earth. He leaves behind him three people, all of whom loved him, one of whom killed him, none of whom had ever seen another person die.

I don't know what Cain imagined might happen when he killed his brother. I don't know that he knew he *could* kill his brother. Maybe he simply thought they'd fight, wrestle until he'd put his little brother in his place. What happened when the blood pooled and Abel's arms went limp and the resistance stopped? Did Cain know this was death? And if he did know, having killed animals before, having seen the life drain out of them, was he terrified to now know humans, too, could die?

Every death is a reminder of all death, the certainty of our coming end. Abel dying was Cain dying. He held his corpse-cold brother, and he held his future self.

Mired in the thick flood of plague-triggered deaths around him, John Donne wrote,

"Each man's death diminishes me,/For I am involved in mankind./Therefore, send not to know/For whom the bell tolls,/It tolls for thee."

And what about Eve, mother of all living and now mother of all dead? How do you keep waking up and getting up and putting one foot in front of another with both sons lost—one killed, one banished, both gone? How do you keep living when you can't stop thinking about your own sin, wondering if somehow this is your fault, if maybe you're the one who opened this terrible door? How do you keep going when you carry your boy's body, buckling under the dead weight, and it feels light in comparison to your guilt?

We don't see Eve grieve in Scripture, not in graphic detail. We don't see Cain grieve, either. The first mourning we see up close on the Bible's pages is Jacob's, when he imagines that his son Joseph has been eaten by wild animals. The Genesis writer records the scene: "Then Jacob tore his clothes, put on sackcloth and mourned for his son many days. All his sons and daughters came to comfort him, but he refused to be comforted. 'No,' he said, 'I will continue to mourn until I join my son in the grave.' So his father wept for him." (Genesis 37:34–35)

Later, King David will also weep for *his* dead sons: once for his not-yet-named baby with Bathsheba, fasting and weeping and praying for some other outcome, not the death inflicted by his own sin; and then again for his son Absalom, his beautiful, kindred-spirit son, the son David rejected and the son who ultimately rejected David, leading an uprising against his own father and dying at the hand of David's army.

When David hears the news of his son's death in battle, he is "shaken." "He went up to the room over the gateway and wept. As he went, he said: 'O my son Absalom! My son, my son Absalom! If only I had died instead of you—O Absalom, my son, my son!'" (2 Samuel 18:33)

Reading the Bible, looking for mourning, I've wondered why the most graphic descriptions of grief are of parents grieving children. I wonder if it's not because God is a parent who lost a child, and those stories are the ones to which He most relates.

When Jesus hangs on the cross, the sky goes black, as if God weeps in ink. At the precise moment of Jesus' death, the earth shakes and the veil in the Temple is torn. And I wonder if that's not God "shaken" like David, tearing His clothes in grief like Jacob.

Is it okay to say I'm glad God grieves? I am. Somehow, knowing that God and I have grief in common, it makes the grief right. Because if God grieves, if death makes even God sad and angry, my sadness and my anger make sense. Fifteen years ago, plunged deep into the pain of loss, nothing made sense. Grief felt wrong. Everything about it made me feel unhinged, swallowed up. I needed someone to tell me I wasn't crazy, someone to say grief is right and good. Someone to sit beside me and tear her clothes and shake her fist at the sky.

I'm writing this book to be that person for you. And to remind you that God is here, too, sad for His children and angry at His enemy, death. Mourning is the righteous reaction of people made to live eternally to a death that steals our destiny.

Yes, God has been victorious over death. And yes, we will one day be freed from its tyranny. *More on that to come...* But here, now, we raise empty hands to the heavens, longing for the people we've loved and lost. Grief is our act of protest, our refusal to let our people go quietly. We grieve together and we grieve together with God, lifting pictures of our loved ones, carving names into marble, lighting candles, refusing to let death extinguish life. If we'll let it, our common grief will be the very thing inspiring us to abundant, rebellious life.

CHAPTER 2

DROWNING

"I am doing what seems the best thing to do… I can't fight any longer."

Virginia Woolf's suicide note.
She filled her coat pockets with rocks and waded into the River Ouse.

Twenty-one-year-olds should not go into meetings at funeral homes. I was reminded of this recently when my friend Tina had to plan her mother's funeral, and then, two years later, her father's. She hated it. Felt helpless and uncertain. Lost. She wished someone else would just make it happen. I sat in a meeting with her, planning the service. How should she know what her father would have wanted, which of his college friends should be pallbearers, what pallbearers were, and whether people would be offended if there weren't any? There were too many things to know. Should she know which casket he would want? Should she know what hymns he liked most? This planning made her feel like she didn't know much about him at all.

But that's not true. We can know people and not know how to answer these questions, not know what kinds of preferences they'd have in every single stupid category. I think of my husband trying to pick out a gift for me at Christmas. He knows me, knows me better than any person on earth knows me, but he stands in the aisles paralyzed by all the choices.

There are too many decisions to make when a person dies. When and where and how and what and who? Who houses the body? Do we want them to embalm the body? Cremate the body? Do we want to donate the body to science? Maybe just donate some organs? Which organs are we okay with donating? What if we wrap them up in a blanket and put them in the ground and plant a tree on top? When should the funeral be? Should we wait for a weekend so more people can come? Should we take a weekday spot and save money? Who's coming? Where are they staying? Who's going to feed them while they're here? Pick them up at the airport? Shuttle them to and from the funeral? Do we advertise the funeral in the newspaper? Who does that? Do we write the obituary or does someone else? What if we want a longer obituary? Do people still read the newspaper? Should we start a Facebook page? Who should moderate the Facebook page? Should we delete the weird thing that girl he used to date just posted? Who decides what does and doesn't get deleted? *Back to the funeral.* Who should preach? Who else should talk? Should we read a poem? Are poems stupid and sentimental? Is there a favorite Bible verse we should read? Who should read it? Who should sit with the family during the service? Does the family sit up front? Should the family enter after the casket or stand up front and shake hands with people as they come in? Or should they shake hands after or should they be shuffled out to their cars? Should we rent a limo? If not, who wants to drive? Should we have a graveside service? Should we release doves or balloons or give everyone a flower to place on the coffin or let whoever wants to help cover the coffin in dirt? What should the tombstone look like? What should it say? Should we scatter the cremated remains or put them in an urn on the mantel? Should there be a viewing before the funeral or cremation? Should the viewing be at a church or the funeral home? Should we sing? Who will sing? What will we sing? Will we have a slideshow with pictures? Which pictures? What song? How do we make one of those things? Which millennial in the family will make the slideshow? Do we include pictures of the ex-wife? Is the ex-wife involved in the funeral planning?

Too many questions.

Especially when the death is sudden and too early. There are no templates for funerals for 55-year-olds without wills who die watching football or for 20-year-olds who die because they fell asleep at the wheel. Funerals are for old people, for people who've had time to plan them.

I've been to the funeral of a man who choked on candy, lying down for a nap. He was single, in his thirties. Healthy.

I've been to the funeral of a teenager who overdosed on heroin. His parents played songs from his iPod, and we all sat in the room listening to rock music looking at a slideshow of selfies in the bathroom mirror.

I've been to the funeral of a two-year-old who died in a car accident, his grandmother behind the wheel, her still in ICU, his coffin the size of carry-on luggage.

I've been to the funeral of a man who fell asleep in his car outside the house after drinking too much and accidentally died of asphyxiation. His two daughters, four and six, sat on the front row. They put flowers on the casket.

When the man at the funeral home with the coffin catalog asked us what Bobby would have wanted, I thought, *He would have wanted not to die*. I tried to imagine what he might have wanted, and found myself imagining things like strapping a parachute on his body and dropping him out of a plane over the ocean.

Bobby wouldn't have had opinions about his funeral because he hadn't had long enough to form any.

We decided on a coffin in a cool charcoal, I think. I can't remember why. Something about his social club in college, maybe. Mom dressed him in the shirt she bought him for Christmas. She had to unwrap it to give it to the undertaker. We agreed to forgo shoes (1) because burying shoes (especially the kind Bobby liked) seemed like a waste of money and (2) because Bobby didn't often wear shoes. We decided to put him in the mausoleum with my grandmother, who'd died when my mom was 24 and I was 8 and Bobby was 7. It seemed to make sense because Mammaw had loved Bobby the most, and because my grandfather had a new wife he loved like he'd loved my grandmother and didn't mind giving his spot to Bobby. We all thought Bobby wouldn't like being alone, though we knew he'd never really know he'd been buried alone. We'd know though. And we knew Bobby wouldn't like it.

One day, when Jesus comes back and gathers the bodies of His children, I figure Bobby will see we put him with Mammaw, and he'll be happy about that.

And honestly, if he's not, I'll tell him he should have made a will.

Recently, I was sitting next to a friend at a folk music festival when she leaned over excitedly to say, "I met someone in a mindfulness club and knew you'd want to meet her—she's a death walker."

You can take a moment to process that sentence.

Turns out "death walker" (in this case) did not refer to some kind of ghost zombie, but rather a normal, living lady who helps grieving people. My friend said this woman walks alongside families after the death of a loved one, helping them make decisions, encouraging them to keep going, explaining complicated processes. She's an advocate, a friend, and an event planner. My friend and I both agreed "grief doula" seemed a better name than "death walker."

The more I thought about this woman—a woman who worked every day in the deep, dark, raging waters of grief, pulling people up, enabling breaths, facilitating survival—the more I thought, *That is too much for any one person.* Right behind that thought came this one: "Does she have a business card?"

If you're reading this because you're grieving, you know the weight of that first tidal wave of grief, the way it hits you and upends you, the way it paralyzes you. It would be advisable to have someone close keeping an eye on things.

About a year after Bobby died, I went on vacation to Los Angeles with my parents. My dad and I surfed on Zuma Beach just north of the city. It's a great beach for professional surfers, but it's a terrible beach for a novice surfer, especially one who hasn't ever surfed without her brother before. My dad and I ended up along the border of Zuma and Westward Beach, a beach so prone to rip currents and "high impact" waves that a lifeguard had famously been paralyzed there, forced into a sandbar headfirst by a particularly powerful swell. *I didn't know these things then.*

All day my eyes stung, wet with salt water—ocean and tears mixed.

I paddled powerfully and painstakingly, and still it took 20 minutes to make it past the breakers. Once I got out there, I pulled every limb onto the safety of the board, afraid if I dangled even a toe off this fiberglass vessel, I'd be eaten by sharks. I didn't know this water. It was darker and deeper, moodier than the Atlantic. Seals played beside us, disappearing and reemerging unpredictably.

Eventually I caught a wave, paddled hard, pushed myself up, lost my balance, and fell off the board, landing in the icy cold water. I managed to grab the board and make it back beyond the waves to my dad. The second wave was different. This time I fell, too—no surprise there—but I fell into the wave, not behind it, my whole body dragged into the curl of the water, like I was in the rinse cycle of a washing machine. Emerging from the pull of the wave, I started kicking, reaching wildly for the top of the water. Instead, unintentionally swimming deeper, I hit my head on the rocky ocean floor.

Sometimes we look back on moments like this and insert what we think we must have been thinking. Maybe that's what I'm doing here. Surely I only had a second to think thoughts underwater, but as I look back at that moment at the bottom of the ocean, what came next feels like a memory, like something that really happened. I remember, vividly, wanting to give up. There in the quiet darkness, upside down, mixed up, I wondered if maybe I could just stay there. Let go. Stop striving. Drown.

The other option—continuing to fight, pushing one more time for the surface, forcing my exhausted limbs to reach and claw—just seemed impossible. I thought, *That's it. I'm done. I can't.* I stopped struggling, and all was quiet.

I'd done this in my bed the day after Bobby died, too. In Bobby's bed, actually. I'd lain there with my eyes closed, trying not to open them, trying to hold onto the darkness and the silence, knowing that opening my eyes meant opening the floodgate, opening myself up to what had happened, to the sting of it all, to the chaos and discord of these pummeling waves of grief.

I lingered in the liminal, holding my pillow and the blanket in clenched fists.

Every morning would be this way. Every morning for a year or more I would wish I could stay in bed, wish I could stay wrapped in darkness and oblivion, wish I could give up on everything that this life without my brother so indifferently required of me. Upside down and mixed up, I wondered if maybe I could just stay there. Let go. Stop striving. Drown.

If Life says, "I can," Death says, "You can't." I couldn't. I couldn't go places, couldn't make choices, couldn't make myself be kind, couldn't get out of bed, couldn't get dressed, couldn't lift my arms for long enough to blow-dry my hair. I couldn't drive without having to pull over because I was crying so hard I couldn't see. I couldn't listen to the radio. I couldn't eat. Couldn't concentrate.

Death's hollow voice chanted, "You can't. You can't. You can't..."

In those moments it seemed like an ocean separated me from the air. Maybe you've been there. Drowning. You know staying down here, underwater, is killing you, but it's also disappearing you and that seems much preferable to doing what it takes to get up and push toward the surface, into the harsh light of unflinching day, exhausted and exposed.

And who's to say you could make it to the surface, anyway? You don't even know which direction is up.

~~~

I'm riding in the car on the way to the viewing, running late because I made my husband stop so I could buy something. A plant. A kind of palm tree I've decided I can't show up without. I got the idea that I needed the palm tree when I remembered that people are supposed to send flowers to funerals. I couldn't image Bobby wanting a bouquet of yellow lilies with stiff white ribbons, so I stopped off at Lowe's, hit up the garden department, and stuffed a palm tree into my back seat. Now I am headed to my 20-year-old brother's viewing, getting poked by palm tree leaves, listening to Christmas music with the windows down while I try to do my makeup.

My hands shake every time I lift the mascara wand.

What am I doing?

I think there are two answers here, both equally true: I am trying. Trying to show up for my family, trying to properly honor my brother who I love, trying to tame the demons inside me, to free myself from their choke hold. I am buying plants and listening to "Santa Baby" and applying blush because, in this flood of death, I am trying to live.

But also, I am pretending. I dab some concealer under my eyes to hide the bags and dark rings. I brush waterproof mascara onto my lashes as if to say, *I've hardly been crying at all.* The blush infuses life into lifeless cheeks.

Later at the viewing, visitation, parade, *whatever you call it*, people will hug me and tell me how strong I am, how well I'm holding up. Ten feet from my brother's coffin someone will say, "Wow. You look beautiful." And as weird as that is to say, it's true. I'm dressed in my favorite outfit. My hair is neat and smooth. I'm wearing red lipstick.
~~~

I feel as if I owe them this. Like it's my duty. My duty to smile and wear heels and look presentable. I use all my air on these efforts to pretend. In the moment, I think this is noble.

When my mother was a young woman and her own mother died, my grandfather gathered the family before the funeral. He told his three sons and one daughter, "We will not act like fools and cry." What he wanted to say was, *We have hope. Don't forget. Our hope can inspire others.* What he ended up doing was forcing my mother to pretend she wasn't drowning.

I was riding in an airplane a while back and the man beside me was traveling for the first time with his one-year-old son. I could tell he hadn't flown on an airplane much himself, either. When the flight attendant approached him and gave the "secure your own oxygen mask first before helping your son" speech, he looked at her like she was crazy. "F*** that," he said to me when she left.

I made a mental note to intervene should we lose pressure in the cabin.

I saw a video of what happens to a person when they lose oxygen. Very quickly we also lose our ability to think clearly. We're alive, but we can't think straight. In this video, the guy who's been deprived of oxygen (for a little under two minutes) tries and fails to use a child's shape-sorting toy. When others ask him which shapes he's holding, he calls a plus sign a square.

We put our own oxygen mask on first not to be selfish, but to ensure we're thinking clearly when we reach out to help others.

Sometimes when you're grieving—I think especially if you're one of the people closest to the point of impact—you feel like a person whose job it is to help everyone around you secure their oxygen masks. Except you don't have one. Soon you're acting nonsensically. Eventually you'll black out.

That's what happened to me. After the viewing and the funeral, after all the trying and pretending, I lost it. And because I had tried and pretended so well, no one knew I was in danger. They went home, left me alone, and there, unseen, I finally ran out of air and gave up.

To this day I wonder if maybe I shouldn't have worn lipstick or pantyhose to the funeral, if an unpainted face or bare legs might have been just the flare I needed. I'm glad I tried to swim. I wish I hadn't pretended I could so convincingly.

My advice to the grieving is simple: Let them know you're drowning. They can't help if they don't know.

Maybe that means you have to acknowledge you're drowning. Maybe it means coming to terms with your inability to handle this alone. Likely it requires a taxing level of vulnerability. Surely it requires humility. Whatever it takes, do it. You are not going to survive this without a savior. Or two. Or ten.

If loss is like a pummeling wave and grief like drowning, then the best way to help a person who's grieving is to jump in the water and pull them up. Mourners—disoriented and exhausted, bullied by death—need lifeguards, people who see death clearly as thief and enemy, people who are alive, capable of breathing, strong swimmers less affected by the wave who can swim for us when we can't. This is what that "death walker" knew.

My friend Martha's first baby was born dead. She told me recently, looking back on that season, "Adulting was exceptionally difficult, especially when such simple tasks as breathing, eating, and sleeping hurt not just emotionally, but physically. Having people help with the everyday things was monumental for us." Drowning people need to be scooped up, carried to safety, shielded from the burden of too many decisions and too many people and too many memories and every sort of expectation.

What does that look like?

It looks like driving to Costco and filling your cart with toilet paper and paper plates and disposable silverware and tissues (real, brand-name tissues), stuff grieving people need as friends and family descend on their homes, stuff they don't have the energy to go to the store and buy.

It looks like dropping off your second vehicle in their driveway so guests from out of town don't have to be ferried around.

It looks like organizing a meal after the funeral and asking as few questions as possible of the bereaved. Just tell them where to show up.

It looks like food. Drowning people don't want to grocery shop or cook. They want to warm up a lasagna some nice lady at church put in their freezer, or order pizza using the gift card a friend sent in the mail. My friend Joy said that when her daughter died, friends delivered a deep freezer to their home, set it up in the garage, and filled it with food.

Saving people from drowning looks like helping them understand what to do with the life insurance money or how to figure out social security or how to end the lease and collect their loved one's stuff.

It looks like cleaning or paying for a maid.

It looks like getting rid of their loved one's porn stash so they don't have to deal with it.

It looks like making a slideshow for the funeral because they don't know how, or sending pictures they may never have seen of moments they might not remember.

It looks like paying for plane tickets to go to the funeral.

It looks like taking their kids for an afternoon so they can sleep or read or take a walk.

It looks like driving their kids to school in the mornings so they don't have to get up and get dressed.

It looks like texting from the store, "Anything you need?" Better yet: "What's your favorite ice cream flavor?" or, "Have you read this book? It's great. I'll grab it and bring it by."

It looks like taking them to the movies for a distraction. Not inviting them to the movies—they'll say no—but rather, telling them you're taking them to the movies. *When can I pick you up?*

It looks like stepping in to advocate for them when other family members or friends less close to the deceased try to get their way.

It looks like being their wingman at church or large gatherings, helping them out of awkward conversations and steering them away from rude people.

It looks like taking over their responsibilities at work or church for a while without complaining.

It looks like spending the night at their house so they don't have to be alone.

It looks like picking up the things sliding off their plates.

And it looks like praying, praying for them and with them, sitting beside them, holding their hands, carrying them to the throne of God, using your strong voice while theirs is weak, asking your all-powerful Father to deliver them in a way you never could.

Too many times we see a person drowning, and we yell

from the shore, "I'm here if you need anything. Just let me know." Do you see that flailing in the water? That's the drowning person letting you know. They need things. Jump in, swim out there, and help.

I didn't drown at the bottom of the Pacific Ocean. My dad was close by and would surely have found me before things went too far. I don't want to be dramatic.

But at the same time, I did think I might drown. I did, for a second, decide I would. And then I decided I wouldn't. I righted myself, pushed off the bottom with my strong—though tired—legs, and quickly felt the sting of spring air on my cheeks, oxygen in my hungry lungs.

I chose to swim that day. Even though it hurt. Even though it meant more chaos and more pain and no promise of finding the surface. Even though drowning seemed like a dream, like some lovely, peaceful escape requiring absolutely nothing of me.

I'd like to say I swam because I was strong. Because I thought of all my loved ones depending on me. Because I was courageous and hopeful and persevering.

But I think, in the end, I swam because I didn't want to die.

This book is, in part, a book about a girl who decided, in the face of death, that she didn't want to die. That's my grief story, and I've had to choose it again and again.

When I moved to Brooklyn, knowing no one, and in one year my dog died and my church back home divided and Justin's grandmother died and we miscarried two babies and lost our funding for the church plant.

When the doctor found a lump in my breast while I was pregnant.

When the other doctor said, "I think you have colon cancer."

When Justin's parents divorced.

When people I loved decided we couldn't disagree and still worship together and left.

When my grandfathers, men who'd raised me, died within two weeks of one another.

Death will not leave a person alone. It sneaks in the shadows, stealing our loved ones, making promises it can't deliver, haunting us, wooing us, breaking us, pushing us into isolation and despair. There is no way to avoid death. Mitigating it, putting up safety rails, putting armor on our hearts only leads to another, more destructive form of death.

I've discovered over the years that every death around me is an invitation to a greater death inside me.

Sometimes Christians think of Death as innocuous, harmless, inevitable, like an annoying puppy growling at our feet, an inconvenience for a moment but then Heaven. *If Heaven is on the other side of Death, how bad can Death be?*

This minimizing of Death causes great tension when we come face to face with it, when we feel the paralyzing pain of loss in our guts and bones, when we confront Death's wrecking henchmen unarmed—despair, anger, apathy, distance... We wonder, "Why am I so sad, when my brother is in Heaven? Why does this loss weigh so much? Why is this current so strong, pulling me further and further out to sea?"

If Death is conquered, why do I feel defeated?

I remember the devastating guilt that came with my grief, the way I struggled to make sense of my pain in light of my hope. Yes, I believed in Heaven. And yes, that brought me immeasurable peace. But the drowning…

If this was God's plan, surely I could learn to accept it with grace and submission. Surely it shouldn't be this hard.

Maybe you feel that way, like your loss is something you should learn to accept and bear up under. I've come to think that's rather like sitting on the ocean floor, the whole Pacific Ocean on your shoulders, surrendered.

What I hadn't wrapped my head around fifteen years ago was the orienting truth that Death is the enemy of Life, the last enemy, according to the apostle Paul, an enemy sentenced to execution (ultimately beaten by Christ's death on the cross), but free for now as if on bail, wreaking havoc. Death isn't God's instrument. Death doesn't fight on God's side. Death isn't God's direct report.

You must know this in the face of loss: Death was never the plan. Death is the consequence of choosing *against* God's plan. God has spent the whole of human history trying to undo this terrible mistake of ours. Even now, He invites us into the Kingdom of Life positioned in armed opposition to the Kingdom of Death.

Death is God's enemy and your enemy, too. It will, without hesitation, swallow you whole if you let it. When you are confronted with Death, when despair threatens to pull you down and never let you up, remember: Death is not a friend. There is no benevolent plan to come to terms with. When you and Death come face to face, the only salvific response is to reach for the power of Christ, grab hold of Life, and fight like Heaven. You cannot surrender.

This Death outside you does not have to lead to Death inside you, but it will if you don't swim. You don't have to swim right away—your brothers and sisters can do that for you. But eventually, you will need to leave the ocean floor and fight the waves.

CHAPTER 3

GATHERED

"Some change at once went through them all, as if this had really happened, and they were all conscious of making a party together... Some weight was taken off them; anything might happen."

Virginia Woolf, *To The Lighthouse*

My brother was one of those people who have friends. Lots of friends. People who'd met him once thought they were best friends, because he made them feel that way. Every one of the cafeteria workers at the college he attended knew his name (and he knew theirs, too). He was the star camp counselor, the guy in the dorm with all the crazy prank ideas, the person who noticed people who other people didn't notice, and the guy who wore a hat a weird way and had every single person in the room wearing theirs the same way within minutes. Well over a decade has passed since he died, and I still receive emails from people who spent just a single day with him and feel like that day changed their life.

I heard Malcolm Gladwell talk about connectors once,

people who draw people together. A connector is the person in a group who brings new people in, the person everyone texts first with news or to hang out. That was Bobby. His niece is just like him. Sometimes I look at her, blue-eyed and blonde-headed, funny and addicted to ketchup and chicken tenders, making friends everywhere, accumulating phone numbers of girls and boys she met on playgrounds, negotiating conflicts between kids in her class, collecting best friend necklaces (she received six last month), and I wonder if my brother has not come back to earth in the form of this child who I love and who drives me crazy because I don't understand her at all.

I have never been a friends person. I want to be. At least I want to want to be. But I prefer sitting alone in rooms reading and writing. Or taking hikes with my one best friend. Or having stirring, aggressive, off-putting conversations with other introverts who don't actually count me as their "friend" because we introverts have stricter guidelines when it comes to determining who's in our very small circle.

Bobby was in my circle. My husband is. My kids. Maybe a handful of friends.

Bobby's circle was the size of the rings of Saturn.

When he died, the entire circle came to grieve. Friends from our college in Tennessee were mostly home for Christmas when the news hit. Some were still taking final exams. They called one another and rented buses to come, drove sixteen hours. Some booked flights. My mom booked rooms at a nearby hotel and called back later to book more.

The entire men's basketball team from our college showed up. Bobby never played on the team, but always cheered (and loudly heckled refs and opposing team players) from his designated courtside seat. At his funeral, these giant young men would sit coffin-side.

When Moses was told that death was near, commanded to climb Mount Nebo, God promised, "You will die and be gathered to your people." (Deuteronomy 32:50) I believe that happened to Bobby, too, that God carried him into the eternal community of the saints, that he came to rest with our grandmother and great-grandmother. But for Bobby, dead before most of his people had even hit middle age, it might make more sense to say that he died and his people were gathered *to him*, his death a call to pilgrimage, an invitation to reunion.

We didn't realize quite how many people would come to Florida until the night of the viewing. I arrived early with my husband and my college best friend, Jules, who was also one of Bobby's many ex-girlfriends (all of whom still loved him to death, beyond death). We set up the room. I tried not to have a complete and total breakdown when my parents told me they'd decided to close the casket and they didn't want me to see Bobby's body, because he didn't look like him and seeing that body wouldn't make me feel any more like Bobby was dead. There was no closure there, they said, and so closed the coffin stayed.

We put a jersey on the coffin, from the club he was in in college. We put his rings on it, and the necklace he always wore. A picture, cropped from a photo of him posing with his favorite band. The picture on the program was of him shirtless, carrying a surfboard. And the incongruity of that, the healthy, good-looking boy, tan and strong in this picture, and the dead body in the coffin—it was too much to carry in two hands. So I put the program down and took my place near my parents as the doors opened and we saw, for the first time, the line of people waiting to get in.

Here's the truth about viewings: They are the worst. Also

the best.

They're the best because they're like one of those episodes of that old show "This Is Your Life," except the person's not there to see his people. Instead, his people get to see his other people, and seeing them brings back memories. All the memories. Viewings are parades of the people who played parts in a person's life. Here's an elementary school teacher. There's the guy he played basketball with in middle school. Here are friends from the show chorus he sang with in high school. There's the girls' volleyball team he managed. Here's his boss from the rec center. There's his Bible class teacher. Here's the lady from church who always told him he did a good job leading singing. There's the girl he dated in ninth grade and the girl he dated in tenth grade and the three girls he dated his senior year. There, up by the casket, are the five girls he dated this year. There were a lot of girls at Bobby's viewing.

All of that, seeing the scope of his short life, all the people who he affected and blessed and charmed and made laugh, that was a gift. I found myself marveling at this long line of people (600 or so by the evening's end), delighted by the stacking up of memories, proof he'd lived, proof he'd lived well, proof my sadness made sense.

But the viewing was the worst, too. Because at a viewing, the people closest to the dead person are the people who host the parade, and every single person who pours into the room walks up to you, hugs you, and, in so many cases, whether or not they intend it, looks to you to help them lift their grief.

There are two ways to hug a person. The first way is to give a hug, to stand tall and welcome another person into your arms. Your arms strong and stable, you pull a person in to give them a gift from the excess of love and confidence and peace inside you. The second way is to take a hug, to fall into another's arms, aching for them to lift you, to hold you, to give you peace from the excess inside *them.*

Most of the hugs you experience as an official representative of the dead at viewings for 20-year-olds who died in accidents are of the second type. You give them more than you receive. This kind of death is too much for people. It's too surprising, too close to home, too upsetting. If Bobby could die, they could die, their child might die, their grandchild. They're sad about Bobby, but it's more than that. They're afraid of death. Or they're angry about death. Or they're just overwhelmingly sad—sad for you, sad for them, sad for the whole cursed earth and every dying person on it. That kind of sadness leaks and sucks, sucks any bit of peace or joy or stability it finds in others.

So while I was feeling okay going into the viewing, feeling loved, stable in Christ, even a little bit at peace, ten minutes in, these people like dementors in *Harry Potter* had taken all I had to give.

They never would have asked for it. They couldn't help but take it.

I remember feeling like Bobby might have been better at this than I was. He liked crowds and people and giving himself up.

Not everyone who hugged me took a hug. I remember the generous hugs that sustained me as the night wore on. I remember the eye contact that said, *I'm here for you*, and these warm, spoken words: "This must be so hard for you. I'm praying for you and rooting for you." Hugs that said, *Here, have some of my strength.* I remember the people who shared positive words about my brother and smiled. The people who laughed as they told a story. I thought it especially brave of those people to laugh in the face of death, to tell living stories like lighting candles in the dark.

Against the wall sat my friend Jules. She arrived with me well before the viewing began and stayed the whole night. I think at some point in the evening she brought me water. Another time she checked in to see what I needed. Looking back, I can't see Jules. I can't remember if she styled her hair straight or curly, if she wore a dress or pants, if she smiled or cried. There are people from that night I remember. A girl who'd known Bobby for a few months who moaned loudly and never left her post at the casket. *God bless her.* A man who hadn't healed from his sister's suicide who gave me a long speech. *God bless him, too.* But there are no distinct memories of Jules—only of a water and being taken care of and maybe a few glances exchanged when the line got held up. I do *remember* Jules though. I remember feeling like one person in the room was there for me and only me, to love me and support me and help me not feel so alone.

A few years ago I had a molar pulled. To this day my tongue wanders back to that spot looking for that tooth, though I have plenty of others. When you lose something, you can't help dwelling on what you've lost. You don't see what you still have because your eyes can't stop looking for what you don't. That's the heart of the lost coin and lost sheep and lost son stories Jesus tells. Yes, you have 99 sheep or 9 coins or one more son, but it can feel like you have nothing and you would do anything to get back what's missing.

When what's missing is a person and when what's missing can't be retrieved, you want all the other persons to notice, to react, to be silent and still in the presence of your mighty pain and in reverence to the greatness of the loss—and by and large, they don't. Grieving people often cannot bear to face the sea of people going about their days as if nothing has happened, as if nothing of value has been lost—co-workers still bustling and emailing and using the microwave, people at church getting coffee and disciplining their kids and laughing about their last vacation, the woman in line ahead of us at the grocery store talking too loudly on her phone and never turning around to tell us how sorry she is about our loss. On the day of my brother's funeral I wanted to stand in the middle of the interstate and stop all the cars, to say, "Hey! I lost my person! Pay attention!"

When I ask friends of mine who've grieved, "What kindnesses do you remember from those first painful days?" some mention food in the freezer, some mention a cleaned house or mowed yard, but most talk about the people who came—people who came to the visitation, people who came to the funeral, people who came by the house to sit quietly or listen. They remember most powerfully the presence of a friend and the way that presence affirmed the magnitude of their loss.

Jesus says, "Blessed are those who mourn, for they shall be comforted." (Matthew 5:4) I don't know exactly what He means. I think maybe He means that mourning opens us up to other people. It makes us dependent on their attentions in the way we always ought to be. Perhaps we're all walking around needing comfort, and it's good to be a mourner because people know you need it and step up. Certainly it's true that mourning people are usually comforted by friends and family. Sometimes they're not, though, and that throws a wrench in things. When the Kingdom is working as it ought, on earth as it is in Heaven, its members will surely find comfort in community, in Scripture, in prayer, and in the indwelling of God's Spirit.

Having experienced that comfort, I can say that it's supernatural. But I can also say—must say—that I'd rather my brother had never died and I didn't need the comforting; maybe not mourning would be a better gift than comfort.

If we have to mourn, if people are going to die whether we like it or not, it's good to mourn alongside others, to have people standing beside us, both holding us up as less-affected pillars and as brothers in grief, comrades in the missing and longing. Paul writes to the Romans, "Rejoice with those who rejoice; mourn with those who mourn." The next words he writes are these: "Live in harmony with one another." (12:15–16) In Ancient Greece, harmony referred to the combination of contrasted elements. In music, that meant a higher and lower note. In the Middle Ages, harmony was the word used to describe two different pitches sounding in combination. I heard a jazz pianist say once that harmony is vertical, a stacking of notes.

When I think of harmony, I think of something pleasing, something lacking discord, but that's not the meaning. Some composers would argue that harmony can be quite displeasing as long as it represents a combination, a partnering, of the high and low.

"Live in harmony with one another" is also rendered this way: "Be of the same mind toward one another," and further, "do not be haughty in mind, but associate with the lowly." Mourning with those who mourn means partnership between those who've been brought low and those who remain high. According to Paul, the only proper response to mourning is collaboration.

I'm thankful, looking back, that I had people who heard my sad song and chose to sing it with me, their soprano carrying my faltering alto on soaring, strapping wings.

It was getting late and the funeral home told us we had to stop taking people because we'd run over our time. The room was full of Bobby's friends, mostly his college friends, the ones staying at the hotel. Grief doesn't conveniently fit itself into two-hour windows, and these kids in this room, none of them over the age of 25, weren't done grieving. They weren't ready to walk away from this coffin and drive to a hotel and go to sleep. My mother knew that. She gathered them like a hen gathers her chicks and said, "Let's go to the beach."

So we did.

We drove to one nearby, piled out of our crammed cars and vans, and sat huddled together facing the pounding waves. A single streetlight at our backs, we stared toward the ocean, indiscernible from the sky, which may as well have been a black curtain on this moonless December night. There we were, 20 or 30 kids plus my parents, land and light behind us, mystery, chaos, and darkness ahead, singing hymns like flares and telling stories, our words like matches and kindling, building a campfire around which we could find warmth and just a little bit of light.

I don't know who started the singing and I don't know who told the first story. I don't remember if this was the plan, if my mother, like a liturgist, had scribbled a makeshift order of worship on the back of a visitation program in the car on the way over. But someone told the first story. And someone else told the second. Soon stories, dozens of them, hung in the air like bubbles blown.

Together these stories worked like a seance, bringing our friend and brother back from the grave. I heard his voice in his friends' voices, and though it was hard, it was the best kind of hard. I'd never have left that beach.

I remember sitting on a blanket holding hands with my husband, laughing while our friend Robbie told a story about Bobby driving backwards through the drive-thru at McDonald's.

No. That's not right. The laughing, yes. But Robbie wasn't *our* friend then. I hardly knew him. We're friends now. I know his children's names. I meet him for dinner when we're in the same town. But then we were basically strangers, bound only by Bobby. Another of Bobby's friends on the beach that night works at the church I work at now. Our daughters are best friends. When the temperature creeps up over 100 degrees we use his pool. But back then, not so much.

What made us friends? I think it was that night on the beach. I think it was coming together to mourn a person we both loved. I think we're friends because, like young people at war, we fought the same enemy and suffered the same loss. And together we fought our way out of the rubble.

Every one of us at that beach that night would walk away on a different path. Some of us would grow bitter and drown our pain in recklessness and excess. Some of us would romanticize the past and forever be comparing a real today to a mostly imagined yesterday. Some of us would heal quickly, mended by the love of strong people close by with time and presence to share. Some of us would struggle to let new friends in because maybe they'd die, too. Some of us would use this grief as an excuse to disengage and drift into despair. Some of us would be transformed by this pain, made better and mighty. Some of us would give in to the pain and let it eat us alive.

I've heard people say that God won't give you more than you can handle. Of course that's ridiculous. It assumes first that God's the exclusive giver of difficulty (what about the forces of evil and death, the principalities and powers we fight against?) and second that He's only asking us to withstand what we're personally able to withstand (what about the power of God to do more than we can ask or imagine?). It seems to me that we're often asked—by God or by Death—to handle more than we can handle. When Bobby died and I was 21 and all his friends were young and new to grief, we were suddenly confronted with a pain we could not handle.

But there did seem to be one possible way to handle the loss, and that way seemed to be *together*. Together with one another and together with God.

We don't always think of grief when we quote Philippians 4:13, "I can do all things through Christ who gives me strength," but handling grief is much closer to Paul's suffering context than winning a football game or getting a promotion. If the power I need to handle what I can't handle is found in Christ, then gatherings like the one on the beach, gatherings of Christ's Body, are invitations for the supernatural, moments for more. That night in particular, I could laugh. I could roundly remember my brother. And I could, for a moment, catch a glimpse of a good and faithful God.

A few months after this moment I will come face to face with the devastation of isolation. I will find myself alone and not together, weakened and weakening. I won't call my parents. I won't go out. I'll sleep all day, isolated even from my own conscious thoughts. But this night I am not alone. I'm listening to stories and holding hands and singing songs—songs *to* God, praise even though, and I'm singing songs *with* God, these holy voices surrounding me, stacked one on top of another, grounding me and lifting me, holding me and leading me onward, toward, beyond...

I think if we could have stayed on that beach, bound, we all might have made it. We'd have held each other and pushed each other and blessed each other and in our connection we would have fought death with conviction and courage, refusing to let it have our hearts. We would have kept singing those songs, sorrow streaming down our faces, joy on our tongues, and victory in our throats.

CHAPTER 4

A GOOD FUNERAL

"A Christian funeral should not be a precious ceremony covering up the fact that someone is really dead."

Thomas G. Long, *Accompany Them With Singing: The Christian Funeral*

I love a good funeral. I've said this before in the presence of my sister-in-law, who thought it an abhorrent thing to say. She looked at me like I'd personally butchered her pet bunny. "Don't say that in front of people," she said.

"Okay," I said. *Maybe she's right*, I thought (though obviously I'm ignoring the advice).

A colleague of mine recently preached his brother-in-law's funeral. The brother-in-law died in a car crash while on vacation in Europe. His wife had been in the car, too, injured severely. Now that she'd recovered enough, it was time for a funeral. The day after the memorial, just before a work meeting, I leaned over and asked, "How was it?" He didn't say "terrible." He didn't say "hard." He smiled and said, "Wonderful."

I wonder if people would be better off knowing funerals can be wonderful.

Bobby's was.

When you walked in the doors of the church on the day we laid Robert David Mays to rest, you were asked to sign his surfboard—that fiberglass altar, our record of names. Today it hangs in my parents' guest room. I lie in the bed and read notes from friends scrawled in the spaces between surf shop stickers. One day they'll take it off the wall and wax it up and let my daughter London use it. She'll take it out into the surf, dive under the waves, and feel close to her uncle (who she's already a better surfer than) and watch as the Sharpie-printed names wash into the sea. But on that day, the funeral day, the names were fresh and the strong smell of permanent marker (permanent!) rose like incense.

At the front of the building, straight up the center aisle, in the same place my father had pulled back my veil, taken my hand, and placed it in my groom's just two years earlier, Bobby's coffin sat, surrounded by flowers (and my palm tree), a black-and-white photo on top of the casket. He wore a hoodie, his shell necklace, and a crooked smile. It's a family trait. Neither he nor I nor my father can smile straight.

Probably there was music while people filed in, muffled talking, and likely an awkward quiet every so often when people felt guilty for the joy stirred up in reunion. We tracked down chairs to place in the aisles, so packed were the pews. My mom made a joke about how Bobby had more people at his funeral than came to my wedding. She laughed, so I think it was a joke.

In attendance were:

Bobby's parents

Three of Bobby's grandparents, all having outlived their grandson

A handful of Bobby's past bosses

Bobby's college president and vice president, who flew in from Tennessee

Teenagers who wanted to be him

Children who'd played with him

College kids who'd lived with him

Past girlfriends but not the current girlfriend (she'd been hospitalized, so strong was her reaction to the news)

Friends of Bobby's parents

Cousins

Church family

And me, Bobby's sister, and my husband, Bobby's friend

No nieces or nephews, none yet born

No wife, none yet procured

No children, none yet conceived

The first person to speak, the one to break the quiet and shush the not-quiet, the person who first stood behind the pulpit and first said words, the person who—in uttering one sentence—made it all real, was my husband, 23 years old, preaching his brother-in-law's funeral. I don't remember what Justin said first, what words he bravely propelled into the void. I think he thanked us for coming, for gathering to remember Bobby. I suspect he told everyone what it meant to the family, *his* family, that they'd come. I don't know how he stood there in those first few seconds of speech except that he knew the prayer was close and if only he could crawl toward the prayer he'd find the strength to go on.

He bowed his head. *Let's pray...*

You hear stories about mothers who lift cars to save their children trapped beneath, or of people who survive for much longer than makes sense in horrific conditions, trying to get home to their families. These inexplicable feats of strength, prompted by love and adrenaline, a most powerful mix, seem impossible. Unless you've been there to see it, and then you say, "It's true. It can happen."

I saw the possible impossible in my husband, one of my brother's very best friends, standing before a room full of devastated friends and loved ones, captaining the ship of our grief and hope, setting a course for healing. I'd see that same possible impossible in face after face as the funeral wore on. It would wear on for three hours.

After the prayer, Justin read Bobby's obituary. At least that's what I remembered until I asked and he said he'd actually read a part of the article about Bobby that had appeared in our local newspaper. The reporter had called and spent an hour with my mom, listening to her talk about what a good boy he'd been, how many lives he'd touched. She wrote a feature with a big picture in the top corner of Bobby with a microphone, singing with his college a capella group. Justin said he'd found two parts of that article especially touching and had shared both. First, the description: "20-year-old Clearwater man." *Is a 20-year-old a man? Had Bobby had the chance to be a man yet?* And second, the part of the article where the author shared the words my mother had said to the policeman when he arrived to tell her the news. Knowing what was coming and unable to accept it, she'd stood on the other side of a closed glass door telling him to go away, he had the wrong house.

Justin said that looking back, he's not sure reading that part of the article showed discretion. I think it was exactly what we all needed to hear as it was exactly what we'd been saying: *Death, you have the wrong house. Go away.*

But of course, despite our pleas, Death took Bobby anyway. And now, at this funeral, there would be a reckoning.

The first movement in a good funeral is acknowledging the loss. Dissonant, chaotic, clanging, the funeral begins with the people mourning, anger and pain on their lips as they cry, *Something terrible has happened. It should not be this way. Death, our sworn enemy, has stolen our person.*

You've seen this part of the funeral before, though rarely is it clearly marked (or well-sung)—it's often the part with the pictures, where we tell stories and remember. We dump our memories on the church floor and wander through them, picking them up one by one, holding them, turning them over, saying to anyone close, "Do you remember, too?"

We do this in part to bring our loved one back to us, as much as we can, if only for a moment, but we also pile up these memories as prosecuting attorneys building a case for the jury.

Did you know this man?

Was he a good man?

Did he live?

Our stories serve as witnesses, our pictures evidence: This person was valuable. He has been taken from us, and our great grief is inevitable and justified.

Together, we prove (and find) Death guilty.

The next movement in the funeral will swell toward resolution. Heaven hangs between the bars of music. Hope is coming. We will be tempted to rush toward it, to rush past the hell, grabbing hope too quickly, eager to skip the distasteful sorrow and the unresolved notes. The unresolved notes, though, are what make us crave resolution, and playing them—acknowledging the pain and devastation, sitting in it for a moment, looking the forces of evil in the eyes—reminds us that a war rages around us, that sin still reigns, at least in part, and that this person in front of us lying in the casket, should he or she be a servant of the most high King, is not victim or victor (not yet, not exactly), but fallen soldier, having bravely fought Death with the power of Life.

Something has been lost here.

Let us take a moment to tally the cost, even just the cost to me:

Because my brother died I will take care of my aging parents alone. Or, should I die too, they may age uncared for.

Because my brother died my children will have no maternal cousins. No brood of blonde-haired babies to pack in a van and drive to the beach.

Because my brother died I will spend the next 15 years trying to make a friend who will understand me the way he did.

Because my brother died I won't sleep through the night for a year.

Those are the costs to me, a fraction of them. With 500 people in this room, how can we rightly enumerate the scale of collective loss? And what about the loss to our cause? What has the Kingdom lost in the death of Bobby Mays? Joy, connection, an earnest soldier devoted to his unit and their mission.

Paul, contemplating death, a man tired of being beaten, isolated, and hated, says, "For to me, to live is Christ and to die is gain." (Philippians 1:21) Gain for him because the pain would stop, but loss for everyone else. Loss for the people who might have heard him preach the truth. Loss for the people being shaped by his example of suffering and faith. Loss to his friends. Loss to the cause.

Death is loss to everyone left behind.

But, Ms. Gerhardt, you might say—you'd say it tenderly,

like a parent helping her child see clearly—*your brother is in Heaven. Everything is better there. I'm sorry for your loss, but this day is a day for celebration.*

No. Maybe sometimes it makes sense for a funeral to be that—when a person dies old and exhausted, entirely used up in Kingdom work. But no. Not in this case. Not in many cases.

I will celebrate at the resurrection. I will celebrate at our reunion. I will give thanks now that my brother is safe and a celebration is on the horizon. But now, at this funeral, my brother three-days-dead, I will measure the hole he leaves in my heart, marking it with tears.

Now, for these few fleeting minutes, we are permitted to wail.

If I had to identify one weakness in the funeral for Robert David Mays on December 16, 2002, at ten o'clock in the morning on Park Boulevard in Pinellas Park, Florida, it would be this: Not nearly enough wailing.

There is a second movement though, an evolution in the funeral song, and I would say we played that movement quite well.

My brother wrote an advice column for our college newspaper. I was the editor. I thought he could use a job, and I knew he was indefatigably funny, so he wrote a column for me in which he gave consistently bad (but hilarious) advice. He wrote about how to shake a stalker and what to do with your problem roommate. He and I argued a lot about that column, mostly about how it wasn't done. He sat in a chair three chairs from mine staring at a blank computer screen, me tossing ideas his way, him telling me how not-funny I was.

For his funeral, I stepped in and wrote a "Dear Bobby" letter in his absence, a letter to his people with advice for living without him, beyond him. I found it this week, rifling through old papers. It's terrible. And lovely. He would have hated it. Sappy. Not funny enough. I wrote it on the airplane the day he died knowing I'd want to say something, knowing I'd want to put words to my feelings, knowing I'd need to talk myself into hope and joy.

I stood up in front of all those people at the funeral and read my letter. I might have cried. I definitely laughed. And for a moment I felt okay.

My dad spoke at the funeral, too. I can't remember what he said. But he wore my brother's coat and hat and glasses. It was tender and funny and a moment when this man who didn't always understand his son inhabited his son. In what must have been an excruciatingly difficult act of vulnerability, my father built a fire around which we all gathered to warm our hands.

Later, people would tell us that our joy had surprised them, taken the air from their lungs, that they didn't understand how we could speak without tears wrecking our words. Were we not sad?

We were sad. Sad like empty balloons. Sad like burnt-out stars. Sad like those penguins who come home after a long hunting season, full of fish for their baby, and find out the baby died in the cruel winter. Sadder than that. But sad wasn't *all* we were. We were also children of God, blessed by God with year-upon-year of time with a beautiful, funny, loving young man. We were sad that the gift had been taken away. Furious at the one who had taken it. But viscerally aware that Bobby had always been a gift.

Others spoke that day. They talked about a guy who'd

loved other people. A guy who never overlooked a janitor, a cafeteria worker, or a lowly freshman. A guy who made you laugh, who never took trouble too seriously. The first guy any of us knew to ever use the text messaging capability on his brick-shaped cell phone. Again and again the story was told, *This boy who died lived well and lives on, lives on in lasting influence and lives on with Christ.* Telling the story of Bobby's life and death and resurrection looked something—a little—like telling the story of Jesus' life and death and resurrection, except Bobby was sometimes a jerk to his sister and Bobby's body was still waiting for the full-on transformation.

Justin, climbing the steps and standing behind the massive, unmoving pulpit, used clearer, more perfect words to define what we'd all poked around at. He reminded us that because Bobby had lived a life like Christ's (in his own small, straining way, the capability a grace), his death would not be forever.

Tom Long writes in his book on funerals, "Every Christian funeral, in its grand and sweeping representation of the journey of a saint toward God, tells a story of majesty. Every Christian funeral is, in fact, a royal funeral."

I hadn't read that book back then. My husband hadn't. My parents hadn't. But we knew that's what Bobby's funeral should be. It did feel royal. It did tell a story. It did represent Bobby's walk with and toward God.

Years later, we'd have people tell us how special that day had seemed, how otherworldly. I'd receive emails from people who chose on that day to come back to God, people who wanted a funeral like this when they died, wanted people to remember something beautiful, wanted the hope of a life that doesn't end. Bobby's funeral, like Bobby's life most days, told the story of the Gospel.

Justin read to us,

> Brothers and sisters, we do not want you to be uninformed about those who sleep in death, so that you do not grieve like the rest of mankind, who have no hope. For we believe that Jesus died and rose again, and so we believe that God will bring with Jesus those who have fallen asleep in Him. According to the Lord's word, we tell you that we who are still alive, who are left until the coming of the Lord, will certainly not precede those who have fallen asleep. For the Lord Himself will come down from Heaven, with a loud command, with the voice of the archangel and with the trumpet call of God, and the dead in Christ will rise first. After that, we who are still alive and are left will be caught up together with them in the clouds to meet the Lord in the air. And so we will be with the Lord forever. Therefore encourage one another with these words. (I Thessalonians 4:13–18)

I did find those words encouraging, just as the apostle Paul who wrote those words expected I might. If I can't have my brother now, there is much peace in knowing I'll be with him again, knowing that though he sleeps for now (Bobby did so love sleep), one day he'll awaken to the sound of a trumpet, and he and I together will be with the Lord forever. I can handle a few years without him, knowing forever is ahead of us.

Eventually the whole room, done listening to truth, ready to join in the telling, erupted in singing, loud singing, sure singing, our voices lifting our loved one into the presence of God. We'd end with a song Bobby sang with his a capella group in college. He sang the lead. The lyrics are a little sentimental and maybe not 100% accurate, but in the song, Bobby sings from the perspective of Jesus welcoming His people home. He sings, "Let me show you around Heaven." And though on that day his friend Derek sang the words, we all remembered Bobby singing them and thought of Bobby perhaps singing them now, of Bobby singing them to us one day.

Nowadays, when my husband is late to dinner or my kids are at my parents' house and my parents won't pick up the phone or when my mom goes in for surgery and it's been too long, I can't help but imagine they're dead. Sometimes, to help myself through the minutes in which I can't know what's happened, the mystery that pushes me to the worst-case scenario, I pass the time by planning their funerals. I've never quite known why this activity gives me peace; it seems morbid and stressful. But as I think back on Bobby's funeral, I realize: perhaps planning the funeral is like telling myself a story.

Long writes, "This is what the Christian funeral is about. Someone we love has died, and so once again we get out our old scripts, assemble onstage, and act out one more time the great and hopeful drama of how the Christian life moves from death to life."

I think it gives me peace to retell the story, to see life and death through the lens of the Gospel truth.

I'm not done talking about this funeral. I want to tell you about putting him in that mausoleum wall. But first I want to say that I know not all funerals are like this, and I'm sorry. I'm sorry that some funerals grope for hope and can't find it. I'm sorry that sometimes the preacher didn't know the person who died and messes up their name. I'm sorry that some funerals don't give you a chance to be sad, that they force you into a feeling you're not ready for yet, a happiness you may never feel. I'm sorry about that aunt you had who made the whole thing about her even though it was your husband who died. I'm sorry about that idiot person who told you how you should mourn and what you should wear and where you ought to sit. I'm sorry that some funerals include tacky poems that tell half-truths about what happened to the person you loved. I'm sorry that for so many people, maybe you, the funeral is a bad memory, one you wish you could shake.

I hate that.

I wish, a little, that I had a bad funeral story, one full of drama or awkwardness. It would make for more excitement and humor in the story I'm telling, and maybe you'd like that better than sentimentality and truth. But alas, my brother's funeral was beautiful. It told the truth about death and the truth about what happens after death. It rang out with hope and thanksgiving. It was a grace, an oasis of grace in what would be, I would soon find out, a Sahara-sized desert of pain, longing, sadness, anger, and despair.

After the funeral in the pink church building where Bobby and I grew up, the very place Bobby had died for the first time twelve years earlier in a lukewarm baptistery with sentimental art painted on the walls, we piled into cars and drove down the street behind the hearse to the cemetery, city police making the way easy thanks to a friend on the city council. Bobby's spot in the mausoleum was toward the back of the property, quiet, off the road, and facing a plaza and a bench. People spilled in haphazardly. There were no chairs. I stood close to the hole in the wall where he'd be placed, remembering the day we'd put my grandmother in that hole, my younger cousin's wail, "Don't put Mammaw in that hole!" He was four.

Today, by contrast, was quiet; no screaming, just sniffling. Quiet until, from up the road, we heard the sound of a bagpipe playing "Amazing Grace" and turned to see one of my brother's friends in full Scottish dress, marching in procession, the casket behind her born by his friends: my husband, that same cousin who'd wailed at Mammaw's interment and now grieved again, Bobby's roommates. These were the men who would have been his groomsmen, all of them handsome, wearing ties and suits, walking through the grass on a beautiful Florida day, all of them absurdly young, most of them older than Bobby had been.

In the church I grew up in, we didn't play instruments in worship. Many of us didn't even listen to religious songs with instruments at home. Every time I'd heard Amazing Grace before that moment (aside from in movies), I'd heard it sung. At church, all 100 of us sang. We sang soprano, alto, tenor, bass. The fullness and humanity, the vulnerability of a capella singing will take your breath away the first time you hear it. It's beautiful. But here on this morning, I was listening to "Amazing Grace" with no voices, and thus, no words. It was like no one could find the words for the moment, like all we could do was moan—not even that. It was like we'd hired this bagpipe to moan for us, like in the Bible when families would hire professional mourners. This bagpipe, a mourning instrument if there ever was one, sang for us and sounded like us, like our tired, broken hearts.

To bury means to conceal, and though we weren't literally burying him under dirt, we were certainly putting him away, out of sight. We did it carefully and lovingly, like I'd tenderly fold a special dress of my daughter's that she'd outgrown, put it in a Rubbermaid tub, and heft it into the attic for safekeeping—for when her own daughter may want to wear it or for when she might want to reminisce, for when she'd need it again. That's what we did with Bobby's body; we put him in a box, and we stored him away for safekeeping, for the time he'd need his body again.

PART 2

Trough

noun:

a hollow between two wave crests in the sea

JANUARY 5, 2003

From the journal of 21-year-old me

All I wanted to do was to touch him. I knew he would be cold. I knew it wouldn't really be him, just what he'd left behind. But still, I just wanted to touch him. Even though Bobby's soul wasn't in that body anymore, there was still a significant part of my brother attached to that tall, slim, tan, knee-scarred body he called home for 20 years. He was so handsome and warm—always warm. I loved his hands—strong and light brown with long, basketball-player fingers, his knuckles oddly shaped and oversized.

I wanted to touch his hands.

Sitting there on that pew, waiting for my chance to touch Bobby, I finally realized it wasn't going to happen. Mom and Dad had told me the casket could be opened before the funeral and closed before people entered the building, but already, an hour before the service was to begin, people were filing into the narrow rows. Maybe after the funeral, I thought. Maybe then I'll get to touch his hands. Maybe then I'll see his body and know this isn't some elaborate joke. Maybe then I'll stop thinking my brother's just at school. Maybe then I'll accept the reality that my beautiful brother is dead.

I never got to touch Bobby. They wheeled him away and into the car before I ever had a chance to say anything. All I wanted to do was to touch his hands. I just wanted to touch my brother before they put him in that cold hole in the marble wall. I wanted to be sure he belonged behind the sterile black letters spelling his name, a name we never called him. Robert. Was Bobby Mays really in that silver box? Were his long fingers, scabby knees, and rough face really there? I don't know. They tell me he was in there, but did anyone check? Did anyone hold his hands? Did anyone touch his weathered cheeks? Did anyone lift up his jeans to double check for rollerblading and basketball scars? I would have checked for those things.

Because I didn't get to make sure, I still don't believe everybody when they say he's not coming back. I know I'm a grown woman. And I know I'm supposed to handle all of this with maturity and fortitude, but all I want to do is get up in front of everybody and yell, "LIARS!" because they have to be kidding me.

I saw the pictures of his car. It was messed up pretty bad, I guess. But I didn't see blood. His seat wasn't torn or bent. The seat was still in perfect shape. If I wanted, I could take it and put it in my car and no one would know it had been in a wreck. So how come my brother wasn't as sturdy as that seat? Why can't I see his blood? Why can't I see him in the hospital with a broken leg or arm or collarbone or something, something you get when you're in a car wreck? Why did my brother die when all of his stuff made it home in one piece? How can I hold his shirt and not hold him? I never thought that his jeans, his rings, his CDs, I never thought those things would outlast my brother. I don't want to wear his ring. I don't want to listen to his CDs. I don't want to wear the sweatshirt he bought me for Christmas.

I just want to hold his hand. I just want to laugh at his jokes. I just want to sit in the same room he's in.

CHAPTER 5

ABANDONED

"Part of his self belonged to her and so would travel with her. Abandoned. That was the word. Enrique [...] was being left behind by Margaret and also by himself, the man she had created out of her love."

Rafael Yglesias, *A Happy Marriage*

I'm in a crowd. People pass quickly. They don't look up. I think I'm in Europe somewhere. Maybe Piccadilly Circus in London. I can't be sure. Car horns blare, people sounds—conversations, taxi-hailing, bags brushing against pant legs—bubble and spill and spike. Until suddenly everything is silence, and I see him. I'm used to this, this thinking I see my brother in a crowd. Sometimes it's a pair of black-framed glasses. Sometimes it's the blonde, spiky hair or the tall, slender build and boyish confidence. Sometimes it's his crooked smile. Always when I see him he disappears into someone else, someone something like him but not him, someone utterly disappointing in their not-him-ness.

This time he doesn't disappear, and I chase him through

the people-packed streets. I chase him for what seems like hours until finally he leads me to a basketball arena. He sits down halfway up the bleachers and puts his elbows on his knees.

I have him.

Now that he's still, I consider my approach. I realize I'm older. He's older. We're full-fledged adults now—not young people learning to be adults, not kids playing house or career. How much time has passed since the last time I saw him? I climb the bleachers without a plan.

I sit beside him. He talks before I say a word, doesn't even turn his head my way, doesn't smile, doesn't raise an eyebrow.

"Hi Jen."

Crushed, the only word I can think to say is: "Why?"

And when he answers, something inside me falls like it's falling from 200 stories in the air, because he says, "I had to get away."

I had this cat named Minerva. She was white and black with a perfect pink nose and the prettiest yellow eyes. I found her in the garage one day, abandoned by her mom. I spent an hour trying to catch her and two weeks trying to tame her. I took her picture on a pile of National Geographic magazines. She couldn't have been bigger than an apple.

For months, Minerva lived in our house and ate cat food and played with toys made of cotton and feathers and bells. She didn't let my husband touch her, but she'd climb into my lap every so often and purr while I petted her pure white neck. On occasion she'd rub her face against my face. I thought she loved me.

One day, Minerva ran out into the yard through an open door. She'd been an inside cat for so long, but being outside stirred something primal in her. She loved it. Came alive. And from then on she wanted to be outdoors. She'd hear the door creak ever so slightly and run from two bedrooms away to sneak out. Eventually we let her spend more and more time outdoors. Soon she was leaving for days at a time.

When she'd come back, she'd be less and less eager to be held. More skittish. More destructive.

I can't remember the last time I got to hold her because I wasn't thinking at the time that it would be the last. It was sometime after her first birthday. We'd thrown her a party, a Quinceanera—because one cat year equals fifteen human years and because Minerva was becoming a woman. We dressed her up in a tutu and tiara. She endured it with a little grace and much contempt.

Minerva ran away a day or two after the party, and we didn't see her again. I assumed she'd been killed by a neighborhood fox. Other cats had. We held a memorial for her and made a photo album with pictures of her time with our family.

That was two years ago.

Last week, leaving the house, driving to dinner, my daughter Eve and I left our neighborhood a different way than we usually do. As we climbed a hill on this less-familiar street, a black-and-white cat bolted in front of us. She was fast, graceful, strikingly beautiful, and I couldn't help but think I'd seen Minerva. I stopped the car, got out, and watched her, searching for some marking to prove to me this wasn't my surely-dead cat. But there was the spot of grey on the extra long tail. I called, "Minerva?" and her head turned, and she took a step toward me.

I sat down. She drew closer, creeping like the wild, nervous predator she'd always been and now was in full. Just two feet away she stopped and stared. I stared back at what was so clearly not a ghost. I reached out to touch her and just as my hand met her soft and familiar fur, she jumped and ran.

I got back in the car and cried all the way to dinner, *abandoned.*

I don't know what happened in the days after Bobby's funeral. I don't know if I flew home to Alabama. I don't think so. I think I waited for Christmas. I must have. Our church in Alabama mailed the Christmas presents I'd already purchased, including Bobby's. I guess Justin stayed with me then. I don't remember.

Grief functions like alcohol when applied liberally, blurring memories, dropping heavy dark curtains over days, even weeks.

I do remember Christmas, or at least part of it. I remember sitting in the living room with my parents, staring at Bobby's presents under the tree, trying to decide what we'd do with them. We'd contemplated not opening any of the presents, but thought better of it, passing out the small, wrapped tokens of love for one another, reminders we weren't alone in this pain. Of course, every present seemed insignificant alongside our great sadness, unable as any one gift was to pile up a commensurate happiness. But any happiness, all happiness was welcome.

Bobby's presents, though—they stumped us. Partly we thought maybe he'd still come back, and if he came back, wouldn't he be upset that we'd ruined his Christmas? Mostly we thought opening the presents would be too sad, calling us back to the moments just weeks ago when we'd shopped for a still-living brother and son.

In the end, we opened them because we couldn't stand them sitting there, taunting us cheerily. Mom had bought Bobby clothes. Dad had probably bought him some toy or tech, I don't know. Justin and I pulled off the candy cane paper, opened the box, and picked up the And 1 basketball shorts I'd found on clearance in exactly his size and favorite color. And 1 was Bobby's favorite brand, way too expensive for his college budget. He had one pair, worn too often, faded and tired.

This was the best Christmas present I had ever given him. And he had rudely refused to show up to receive it.

Recently, at a writing workshop, my writing coach asked me to think back to my earliest memory, to write about what I could see, what I couldn't see, what I heard, felt, tasted. My earliest memory has always been of going to the hospital to see my baby brother. I told my parents I remembered the elevator ride and the doors opening, that I remembered a poster with a picture of a baby. My parents said the poster was of Bobby, that he'd been "NICU baby of the month." Bobby was born too early, almost cost my mother her life, almost died himself. But he lived instead and stayed in NICU at All Children's Hospital for weeks.

Lately, I wonder if the memory is made up. In the memory, I'm low, knee-high to the adults around me, but I wonder if I'd have been walking at 17 months. Seems like someone would have held me. I wonder why I would have remembered the poster and not actually seeing my brother, tubes inserted in his head and arms and legs, machines whirring around him like ministering angels. I am uncertain of this memory. And also certain that my first memory would surely have involved my brother.

I cannot recall a life before him.

I have another memory. I think I'm four or five. It's dusk. I hear crickets and smell smoke. The air is heavy with water. I'm in a bathing suit standing on the dock reaching out over the Weeki Wachee River. We live here on this river. My parents are caretakers of a camp. This water on my lips tastes like my home. In the memory, my dad lights a firework and we throw it into the water and watch it swim. This is a miracle to me, fire and color alive when it should be drowned. I have to look this up as an adult to make sure it's real and possible. Even looking back, it seems a marvel. As I root around in the memory, trying to see and hear and taste, I look for Bobby, and though I don't see him, I feel him there. He's at my side, shaking the water from his thick, wet hair, throwing fireworks too close to fish, joining me in the wonder and joy of an evening like this, everything electric.

Tomorrow we'll swim, I'll tow his four-wheeler with my bike when it runs out of power. We'll take care of the puppies, maybe name them. We'll pretend to be He-Man and She-Ra. We'll reign as king and queen of this not-so-small kingdom in the marshland of Florida, palm frond as scepter, seaweed as crown.

I comb through the memories looking for Bobby, and in almost every one he is there. We ride bikes to the 7-Eleven together. We play school under the dining room table. We watch *Saved By the Bell* on TV. We ride to high school together, on the bus and in my car. We skip school and go to the beach. We work together at the mall. We sing together in chorus. We go to college together. He is the best man in my wedding. He convinces my coach to pull me out of a college intramural football game because he heard from a friend of a friend that I might be pregnant (I am not). He sleeps on my couch while I entertain yet another of his girlfriends. He visits our first house and is the first person to sleep in our guest bedroom. He leads singing at our first church as preacher and preacher's wife, and the little girls in my Bible class fall in love.

I have never lived without Bobby Mays. I don't know how to.

I did go back to Alabama after Christmas. And then my parents called and asked if I'd go with them to New York City. Mom had always wanted to go to New York City. She and Dad both had time off of work, and they were hoping to find some distraction that might keep their minds off the breath-robbing pain; lying in bed all day crying was wearing on them. Plus, New York had the added bonus of our not knowing anyone there and Bobby's having never been there. We wanted to be alone and distracted and not looked at with pity, so we went to New York and stayed in Times Square and stood on top of the Empire State Building looking for perspective.

I took pictures on black-and-white film.

Our first night in the city, we checked into our room and fell on the beds, exhausted. Just getting there had taken every ounce of energy we had. But then we looked out the window and saw flakes falling, easy to see against the black steel of the closest building. I put on my coat and convinced my dad to come with me, and we stood in front of our hotel looking at snow.

We bought tickets to a play from the TKTS booth, because a Broadway play seemed like what you do in New York City. We picked *Les Misérables* because I recognized the title. My memories from the play are blurry and episodic—uncomfortable seats, a revolving set, being in a balcony, and crying. *Les Mis*, it turns out, is a play about dying. Every major character dies, almost dies, holds someone while they die, or sings about dying. Of the people who die in *Les Mis*, all of them are too young. Toward the play's end, exhausted of weeping and unable to stop, I watch the young man Marius holding a dying Eponine, just a fifteen-year-old girl, and I hear my dad—my dad who's never seen a play like this before, my dad who drives a truck and hunts and fishes and doesn't cry in public—I hear him two seats down, wailing like a wounded animal.

We are blindsided by this play about dying. It seems death is taunting us, like Achilles dragging the lifeless body of Hector around Troy, Hector's whole family forced to watch.

There is no running away from death.

The Psalmist wrote, "A horse is a vain hope for deliverance; despite all its great strength it cannot save." (33:17) Similarly, a trip to New York City.

After the play, standing outside the theater, all of us exhausted, eyes red and puffy, I apologized for suggesting the absolute worst play for the moment. My dad laughed. He said, "I kept waiting for those gay guys next to me to give me a hug."

This trip to New York is the first trip I have ever taken with my parents without my brother, and at every turn his absence haunts. We can't be the three of us without missing the fourth. This sad trip to this cold place is the first in what will be an entire future of Bobby-less vacations. Never again will my brother and I run off to explore or wander while my parents sleep in. Never again will Bobby whine from the backseat or fall asleep in my space or complain about the artsy-fartsy thing I want to do.

This feeling I get watching my parents walk together while I walk alone is new and terrible. In this family, I am missing my pair. I will always be missing him. Everything feels wrong and broken.

In the book of Ruth, I see Naomi tell her daughters-in-law, "Go home. I can't have any more sons for you." And I think about how crushing that must have been for Naomi to say, knowing, in her own poverty of partner and potential, she has nothing to offer these girls. I look at my own parents who can't have any more siblings for me, how crushed they must be watching me sit alone across the booth at dinner.

There will be no more brothers.

MY INHERITANCE OF ABANDONMENT, A LIST:

Six Things My Brother Left Me When He Died

1. The crushing weight of my parents' expectations.

I haven't called my parents in a week. This is the kind of thing I often do, not because I don't love them but because I am distracted and distractible. I am the kind who falls down rabbit holes and sets off on adventures without her cell phone. In this grief, I never want to talk to anyone. But my parents lost one child and they grab at me, their lone heir, like I'm the chicken line in our sea-tossed boat. I'm not cut out for being held so tightly.

Bobby liked being held. Bobby was the kid who was moving home. Bobby was the one who was loyal and care-giving and liked traditions and holidays and hanging out. He stayed up late talking to mom on the couch. He begged her to make him chicken and dumplings. I was the kid who achieved stuff. But also the one who moved away from home and didn't call enough and never remembered important family events. Together, my brother and I made our parents happy and proud, respectively.

I am capable of making them proud without him. I feel incapable of making them happy.

2. A wrecked husband.

Before Bobby left, my husband was whole, and now he is part missing. We have been married for two years and change—not long. We live in the middle of a field far away from home and mostly just know each other. I have known Justin to be emotionally stable, hard-working, and driven. Today we are lying on a couch with the lights off, ice cream cartons, pizza boxes, and empty bottles of Diet Coke on the coffee table. The TV glows with what? Probably some TLC show I convinced him to watch. We're like addicts strung out on the slow drip of distraction, our grief dulled but still heavy, anchoring us to this oversized piece of furniture. One of us should get up. One of us should go to work. One of us should clean up the pizza boxes or pay the bills or wash dishes. One of us should be stronger so the other might be weak.

I am mad that Bobby abandoned me. I am furious that he took half of my husband.

3. No cousins for my kids.

Though I don't currently have kids, I will have kids. I will have two girls, one of whom is Bobby's twin, and both those girls will grow up without a single cousin on my side of the family. And though I love the other side of the family, there is something special about watching your brother's kids play with your kids, something wondrous about taking them to the river you fished in together, about teaching them games you played, about riding bikes and telling stories about the time you tied their dad's skateboard to your bike and you dragged him down the street without knowing he'd fallen forward and you realized it too late and looked back to find his precious little face covered in blood and then had a meeting to figure out how to hide it from mom.

I grew up listening to my uncles tell stories about jumping off bridges into the river and playing with quirky neighborhood kids and collectively fearing my grandfather. I have stories. *I wanted to tell stories...*

4. No one to call me on my crap.

Sometimes I remember things wrong. I remember my parents being more strict than they were, my church being less accepting. I remember my childhood as more trying, my clothes less cool. And at every turn into misremembering my brother was there to call me out. "You always had better clothes than me," he'd say. "You loved our church," he'd tell me. "Mom and Dad let you get away with everything."

And he'd be right. I was wrong.

Now I'll be wrong and not know it.

5. The responsibility of taking care of my parents as they age.

When my mom gets thyroid cancer in a few years, as she will, I will drive from Texas to Florida and sit in a doctor's office, waiting, wondering why my good-for-nothing brother isn't here to help. I will inevitably feel this again when they are older, less capable. When I am loving them with all I have but feeling too small for the task and knowing I shouldn't be doing it alone.

6. The responsibility of burying both of my parents alone.

Assuming I outlive them, I will plan at least one of my parents' funerals alone. If it's my mom's, I will have to smuggle her ashes into the state of New York and discreetly scatter them in Central Park—discreetly so as to avoid arrest. If it's my dad's, I'll be on a boat in the Gulf, sun setting, waves rising and falling, ashes sticking to my clothes because scattering remains is never as clean or romantic as it seems in movies. Either way, I will be wondering where the heck my brother is.

There is no overestimating the pain of abandonment. It's like waking up to find your arm missing; a piece of you is gone. Daniel Wegner, in his research on what he calls "transactive memory," determined that we often store things in the minds of those we love and live and work with. You choose not to memorize a phone number because she knows it and you can ask her. You never learn how to reset the router because he always does it. You seem nicer than you actually are at parties because her joy and charm always cover up your impatience. Malcolm Gladwell, reflecting on this phenomenon, said it's like "little bits of ourselves [live] in other people." When a loved one dies, we lose our friend and our self. When my brother died, I became a different, lesser person.

I knew, on paper, he didn't choose to leave, but feeling

his loss so keenly, I couldn't help feeling like he had, like he wanted to get away from me. I didn't have words for this feeling early on. I just thought I was sad and mad. It's only been recently that I've landed on that word: abandoned.

I've been reading the book of Jeremiah lately, listening to God mourn, realizing that God, the sovereign Creator God, felt abandoned. Jeremiah and Lamentations both reveal God's grief, communicating in graphic detail what it feels like for someone you love to go away and refuse to come back. God says to Jeremiah, "If My head were a flowing spring, My eyes a fountain of tears, I would weep day and night." (9:1)

God, of course, was actually abandoned. All His people turned their backs on Him. No one, save Jeremiah, would even listen to His tired, heavy, emotion-thick voice. God was alone, unloved, rejected.

Maybe you're reading this book and you have more reason to feel abandoned than I do. Maybe the person you loved and lost left you before they died. Maybe they'd stopped trying to love you even as you loved them. Maybe they died by suicide and you can't shake the feeling that they just wanted to get away from you. I can't speak to your pain with authority or experience. You're probably feeling that right now, listening to my simple story and saying in your head, "You have no idea, girl." You're right. I don't. I'm sorry. Maybe you'll find some comfort in knowing God's been where you are. And maybe it'll bless you to know that when God felt abandoned, He did a lot of crying.

Now is the point in the story where something good happens and I'm reminded I wasn't truly abandoned, the point where

I talk about how God never abandoned me and about how I found myself surrounded by people. That's the expected turn, and honestly, I intend to take it. It may seem sentimental, but it's the truth, and you, in your pain, need truth. And hope.

But before I dip into the light, I want to tell you another truth: this feeling of abandonment—it doesn't exactly go away. I know people who still feel abandoned 20 years post-loss. For me, though, the abandonment has shifted shape over the years, morphing into a kind of longing. Today I rarely get angry at my brother for leaving. But I do, upon facing yet another consequence of his absence, often long to go where he is. I've realized that this feeling, this desire to be with my brother, is homesickness. I don't want him to come back. I want to go where he is. I want to go home.

After my brother died, my parents called and invited me on a trip to New York City. We got a hotel in Times Square and saw a play and went to the Metropolitan Museum of Art. I told you that already, but I only told you half the story. I told you about the sad parts, about how much we missed Bobby, about how much we cried, about how cold it was. What I didn't tell you was that my parents, in their grief, thought of me and wanted to be with me. They went to the play I wanted to see and spent three hours in a museum they didn't care for, because they loved me, because they were with me.

There in New York with my parents, feeling our loss like lead, I wasn't solely aware of what I was missing. I was also reminded of what I had, of these two parents still here, still loving me and one another, still devoted to living, refusing to give up. We ate cheesecake and greasy pizza together. We went to the zoo, and my dad hoisted me onto his shoulders so I could get a better view of the polar bears. I remember watching my mom and dad walk, holding hands, down the Central Park Mall, 40 and 42 years old, thinking how brave they were.

It would be hard to deal with this loss together. In the months to come we would argue and disappoint one another a hundred times. But it would be easier to deal with this together than to deal with it alone.

When I got home to Alabama and I sat in my little house with my beautiful husband, crying on a couch, I couldn't help but be grateful for this partner in grief, someone with me and for me, someone with whom to bandage wounds, someone with whom to embrace distraction, someone with whom to imagine a new future, someone to call me out and up, someone to hear the alarm in the morning and push me out of bed, someone to pray over me and lift me off the floor.

And it wasn't just my husband and my parents around me living and inspiring me to live. I had church people and Bobby's friends and my friends, people who wrote letters, shared kind words, told stories, and helped. All around me, people pushed their way into my life, saying, "We're here. You're not alone."

I did feel abandoned when Bobby died, but I also felt surrounded.

I write and speak a lot these days (these days on the far, far side of loss) about joy and sadness, about looking for God even in hard times. I teach Bible classes on it and give speeches to my kids about it. I've realized how important it is in seasons of pain to try and see, to climb up to a high place and seek perspective, to open your eyes not just to the darkness but also to the light. If we're not careful, in our grief (for example), we'll begin to think everything is darkness. Grief has a way of blinding us.

There's this prayer in the book of Nehemiah that I find instructive as I navigate hard things and seek to see clearly. Nehemiah, reflecting on his own difficult circumstances and on Israel's history with God, prays, "Because of Your great compassion You did not abandon [Your people] in the wilderness. By day the pillar of cloud did not fail to guide them on their path, nor the pillar of fire by night to shine on the way they were to take. You gave Your good Spirit to instruct them. You did not withhold Your manna from their mouths, and You gave them water for their thirst. For forty years You sustained them in the wilderness." (9:19)

You did not abandon Your people in the wilderness. *Beautiful.*

What I find so interesting about this passage is the way time brings clarity and wisdom. Nehemiah lives generations after the wilderness wandering. When he looks back at his people's history, he sees a God who was faithful, a God providing generous and loving care in the middle of a very hard thing. But that's not exactly how it felt for Israel in the midst of it all. For 40 years they lived in the desert, tired, frustrated, sick of eating the same two foods every single day. They wanted meaningful work, a plot of land to call their own. They wanted homes, something to leave their children. They wanted purpose and comfort. Again and again they complained to God, disobeyed God, or forgot God. I think they let the darkness blind them to the light.

Nehemiah, though, he can see clearly, and he knows, even in the wilderness, God was there. In fact, in the wilderness, God was present in more remarkable, more powerful, more visible ways, ways Israel never experienced in the comfort of the promised land—a fiery pillar, a cloud of presence, split seas, manna and quail.

You did not abandon Your people in the wilderness—that's been my experience. When things have been most broken, God has been most real. He's real all the time, right, I know. But when Bobby died and all the lights in all the world were snuffed out, it was then when I most needed the pillar of fire.

Sometimes just being in the wilderness convinces us we've been abandoned. Surely God isn't *here*. But if we'll look we'll see His presence lighting and warming and leading with blazing certainty. When I felt most abandoned by Bobby, I felt God's presence most powerfully. It's like the loneliness opened my eyes, like the dark helped me see.

What does it mean to say, "God did not abandon me in the wilderness?" It's lovely, but perhaps empty. Did I simply lean upon an invisible crutch until my hurting healed? Or did I somehow actually experience God?

I know this…

Reading Scripture after Bobby died felt like drinking water after a too-long run in the southern heat. I guzzled and was revived. God's words felt alive, reaching inside me to re-order my parts, quiet my fears, and widen my perspective. The Bible was a comfort and a light in my pain.

Worship aligned the compass of my heart, leading me toward God instead of away from Him, calling me close in my vulnerability even as I all I wanted to do was hide. Worship was like sitting down to tea with a friend and Father. It felt safe. Too, worship was like cutting open my wrists and bleeding out, not safe but visceral and revealing. Each time, God would clean up the blood, provide a transfusion of Christ's for mine, and send me on my way.

Prayer became honest and selfless. In my pain, God led me into the pain of others, calling me to pray beyond myself and then act in response to my prayers.

The church transformed from place to people, from event to practice. I saw God in the seven-year-olds I taught on Sundays and the widows I drove to lunch and the elder and his wife who welcomed us into their home and loved us like parents love their children. In this season of grief, I learned how to receive love.

It seems featherlight to say God was here because I saw Him and then not provide DNA evidence. But I believe He was. And His presence, His healing and comfort, His guidance and love, stood as a daily reminder that I wasn't alone. That though every person I love were to leave me, He'd stand beside me, a cloud and a flame, lifting my head.

When I look back at my "Inheritance of Abandonment," as I consider, line by line, the extent of my loss, I'm reminded that the loss isn't total and the loneliness isn't complete.

When I feel my parents' disappointment, God is here to remind me I'm enough.

When my husband is broken by grief, God is here to speak words of comfort.

When my kids don't have cousins, God is here providing, filling their Bible classes with little girls just their age, filling our home with friends like aunts and uncles.

When no one is here to call me on my crap, God is here and quite willing to hit me over the head with truth, taking me to task.

When my parents get old and need constant care, God will be here with daily bread, enough love and power to press on, all the help I need.

And when my parents die, God will be the one standing beside me on the boat, lifting my eyes to a better, more real world just beyond the horizon, reminding me this is just a shadow.

JANUARY 6, 2003

I am so confused right now. I have no idea what to do with myself. All I want to do is get over this, work through it. But at the same time all I want to do is to sit on my couch or lie in my bed doing absolutely nothing but wallowing...

I'm not sure how I'm supposed to let this experience affect me. In reality it's only made me sad and sick. I hurt every day when I wake up and every night until I finally fall asleep. Sometimes I forget that Bobby's died for a second but am forced back to reality by the aching pain in my chest and the sharp pain in my stomach. My head aches dully all day and my muscles feel sore... There's no pill to make this hurt go away. Nothing makes me feel better, not a hug, not a card, not good memories, nothing.

I have to go on with life and act like a normal individual. I can't just sit around and think all day about the fact that my favorite person to play with got in a car accident and died. I can't just cry all the time...

Maybe it doesn't matter what I do. Maybe nobody cares if I'm strong or weak or whatever. I'm sure some people think I should probably be over it already. I mean, hey, who's really that close to their brother anyway?

CHAPTER 6

ANGRY

"Anybody can become angry—that is easy, but to be angry with the right person and to the right degree and at the right time and for the right purpose, and in the right way—that is not within everybody's power and is not easy."

Aristotle, *The Art of Rhetoric*

It's January. The air is cold, and the year is new. It's the first year in which my brother will not have lived a day. I'm gathered with my family at my grandfather's house to watch the Fiesta Bowl. My football team, the Miami Hurricanes, is playing the Ohio State Buckeyes for the national title. Last year we won the championship matchup, and we haven't lost a game since—a perfect season.

I love football. I grew up watching the games at my grandfather's house, rooting for the Hurricanes, making posters, painting my face, decorating my bedroom in green and orange. My brother rooted for the Florida State Seminoles with the same kind of fervor, and in the early nineties, our most formative years, the Seminoles and Hurricanes were at the height of a heated, thrilling rivalry. In rooting against each other, Bobby and I drew close to one another. Saturday football games bound us.

Because of that, this isn't easy—sitting here with my parents and grandfather and cousins watching this nail-biter of a football game. Bobby's sarcastic voice is noticeably absent. I wonder if he'd have rooted for Ohio State just to get under my skin. It's unlikely because the Hurricanes beat FSU this year (a game he was alive to see and yell through). If his team had to lose to Miami, Miami had better be the best team in the country.

To say I am involved in this football game is an understatement. Tonight I have dumped every bit of emotion in my body onto the backs of these two teams. I am clinging to the Hurricanes and their proven excellence for just a taste of joy, a glimpse of victory. And I am projecting onto the Buckeyes, those red jerseys like red capes to a bull, all of my anger.

At halftime we are behind by seven, and I cannot talk to anyone in the room. I stand at the edge of the hallway for the entire fourth quarter and first overtime, fists clenched, afraid I'll make a fool of myself if something goes wrong, eager to be out of eyeshot in case I start crying.

We score first in overtime, meaning Ohio State has to score a touchdown to win. On the five-yard line on fourth down, Ohio State's quarterback throws an incomplete pass.

Game. Over.

Miami fans rush the field, and I start praying. I thank God for this tiny victory, for this moment when the right thing happened. I am so tired of loss. So tired of being robbed. Praise God; the Miami Hurricanes have beaten the clearly inferior and undeserving Buckeyes.

But then—with half the stands emptying onto the

grass—a flag. The announcers had missed it. The crowd had missed it. A ref (not the ref closest to the play) has called pass interference.

I lose my mind.

I watch the replay and, unbiased as I obviously am, I see zero offense. I yell at the screen to say as much. My whole family does. The announcers watching can't believe the call. The coaches erupt. The stadium goes bananas.

This call will live on in infamy as one of the most controversial play calls in NCAA football history. You can find it online—videos, articles, arguments. If this call hadn't been made, the Miami Hurricanes would have been the 2003 National Champions. Instead, the Buckeyes grab momentum from the dumbfounded Hurricanes and win in a second overtime.

This loss, as small as it certainly is, on the heels of the biggest loss of my life, is too much. It's like I was robbed, left with only the shirt on my back, and then someone came for my shirt. This isn't true of course, but it's how I feel. I leave the room full of rowdy, disappointed family members, walk down the hall to the guest bedroom, turn out the lights, and climb under the covers of the guest bed. My husband will come in later and take me home.

For the next fifteen years I will hate Ohio State with the white-hot fire of indignation.

Counselors and authors and grief-expert-people say anger is one stage of grief. I knew that before Bobby died, but after Bobby died, I get it. I'm not an angry person, normally. I don't hold grudges. I forgive quickly. I don't have high expectations of others. But in grief, I find, I feel owed.

In his book *Enemies of the Heart*, Andy Stanley says, "The root of anger is the perception that something has been taken. Something is owed you." When your little brother dies before his 21st birthday there's no "perception" that something's been taken. Something *has* been taken. And you can't get it back. This grief anger I feel is consuming, creeping, and compelling.

In those early days of writing an obituary and making a slideshow and shuttling his never-ending list of friends around town, I am generally angry at the whole world. Other worlds too. I am angry about everything. Angry at the people next to me on the road, driving and dancing to music like life is great. I'm angry at the fishermen lining the bridge I drive across back and forth from my parents' house to the airport, sunshine and smiles on their cheeks, peace in their posture. I'm angry at the radio DJs, loud, obnoxious, irreverent.

More reasonably, I'm angry at the person who invented cruise control despite the fact that people might leave it on and fall asleep and drive into trees. I'm angry at Bobby for driving tired when he knew he was terrible at driving tired, angry at myself for not driving up to see Bobby more these past few months…

Weeks and months after the funeral, I'm angry about not being able to call Bobby when I'm having a hard day. I'm angry about my lack of focus when before I achieved it so easily. I'm angry about my new fear of long-distance driving, something I always loved.

I don't know who to blame for these thefts. It isn't Bobby's fault he died. A little, maybe, but mostly it was an accident, the kind of error in judgment 20-year-olds make all the time and live to talk about. For a while, though, I am furious at him—furious at Bobby in Heaven sleeping comfortably in the presence of God while I toil away down here in this busted place full of sadness and longing.

I am furious at Bobby for a long time.

And then one day I decide not to be. Because there's nothing he can do now to fix what's been broken.

I also decide to stop being mad at myself, because it isn't my fault I didn't visit Bobby at college more. Newly married and fresh out of school, Justin and I barely had money to buy groceries. And even if I could have gone, even if I should have, what then? What can I possibly recapture with this fury? Fires destroy; they don't reclaim.

I realize I can't be angry at all the people who're still happy; they owe me nothing. And who am I to begrudge them their fleeting happiness, their temporary state of not-grieving?

I even start feeling like I can't be angry at the Ohio State Buckeyes. It's not their fault a ref made a bad call and my team lost three weeks after my brother died. It's nice to have an effigy, but it's also dishonest. It's not the Buckeyes I hate.

I run through the list of offenders, potential points for fury focus, and find no person to blame. I'm not angry at anybody. But I'm still angry. So angry.

Surely *someone* is responsible for this ceaseless, titanic pain. Who can I blame for this worst thing? Who can you blame for yours?

Maybe we can blame God.

Before my brother died, I held these things to be unquestionably true:

1. God is real.
2. God, my Father, loves me and wants good for me.

3. God hears my prayers.
4. God is in control.

But then, one cold winter morning, with every bit of faith in my bones, I prayed for God to save my brother. And in seconds I received a phone call to let me know He hadn't. The proximity of the answer to the ask knocked my feet out from under me. Or maybe it shook the very ground on which I stood.

It's cliché to go through a hard thing and shake your fist at God. Bad things happen to *me*, and suddenly maybe God isn't good. Somehow I didn't notice all the bad things happening all around every day to other people. I get it. It's selfish. But nevertheless, grief often takes us to the edges of our faith. It forces us to take another look at this God fellow.

Is He safe?

Is He kind?

Is He capable?

Is He good?

Is He?

In grief, these questions bubble up and around persons of faith, engulfing us in foggy, imprecise doubt. Instead of poking at the questions, instead of doubting the doubts, seeking wisdom and clarity and light, we usually choose to make camp in the twilight of confusion, to live in the fog for a while. It seems easier, and we're tired.

After Bobby dies, as the months roll on and the pain grows and the anger mounts, I choose the fog. If God is in control and my brother still died, I will be angry at God. It's His fault. He doesn't love me. Or He doesn't answer prayers. Or He's not really that powerful. Or He's selfish with His power. What kind of God sits around watching boys die for no good reason? Eventually I begin to doubt God's very existence, but I find doubt dissatisfying. I can't quit faith, because I want someone to be mad at. The worst thing I can imagine is not having someone to blame.

I'm at Barnes and Noble when I see Philip Yancey's newest book, *Disappointment With God.* I pick it up, the title a mirror. God has let me down. I had expectations, and those expectations have not been met, so I'm disappointed. Disappointed with a heaping side dish of "You owe me." I read this book in the car on a road trip with my husband and it makes us cry and it makes us confused and at least once we throw it down. But then we pick it up again.

Yancey writes about a God who defies categorization, a God much more complex than the one I thought I knew. Yancey looks at the God of Exodus who releases the plagues, speaks from a fire, and sics snakes on people who whine. He looks at the God of John who brings light, life, healing, and love. He looks at the God of David who sometimes seems far away. And He looks at the God of Job, a God who tests a guy who doesn't know he's being tested. When God takes everything Job cares about—his wealth, his health, his kids—Job maintains his faith (but not his composure). Angry, *owed*, Job launches into a chapters-long rant, refusing the counsel of friends, accusing God of injustice and unkindness. Job says all the things I feel and won't say out loud. Yancey says, reflecting on Job's reaction to the upending of his understanding of God,

One bold message in the Book of Job is that you can say anything to God. Throw at him your grief, your anger, your doubt, your bitterness, your betrayal, your disappointment—he can absorb them all. As often as not, spiritual giants of the Bible are shown contending with God. They prefer to go away limping, like Jacob, rather than to shut God out. In this respect, the Bible prefigures a tenet of modern psychology: you can't really deny your feelings or make them disappear, so you might as well express them. God can deal with every human response save one. He cannot abide the response I fall back on instinctively: an attempt to ignore him or treat him as though he does not exist. That response never once occurred to Job.

It occurs to me, as I read, both that I have decided God can't handle my anger and that I am trying to punish God by ignoring Him. I decide to try Yancey's suggestion and Job's example and begin talking to God this way. Honestly.

I don't remember the first time I pray this way, but I do remember standing in my driveway in the dark, cows mooing in the distance, a dog barking, a sky dusted with stars, me telling the God who made it all how mad I am at Him. It's a strange thing to yell at God. It feels wrong. It grows on me though, and it doesn't take long for me to finally get around to what I most want to say: "God, You had the power to save my brother, and You didn't, even though I asked You to. You don't love me like You say You do."

It feels good to say this to God directly. I say this and so many other things I feel.

Speaking my mind is like pouring out the contents of my purse. Once I see things there on the table, out in the open, extricated from the dark corners and folds, I reconsider their value. Some of the things I say to God are ridiculous. Some things are unfair. Some things are clearly the product of a faulty foundation. Some are legitimate and unnerving. I decide I have a case and begin assembling evidence for God's failure. I make lists of the ways God has disappointed me. I read Bertrand Russell and others arguing for a Godless world. I lay out my reasons, and though they are compelling and emotionally satisfying, they're also not completely compelling and not entirely emotionally satisfying. As my doubts grow, somehow my faith does too.

I think about what I'd say to defend God against these kinds of accusations, and I start grilling my doubts, subjecting them to the same kind of prosecution I'm making God endure. I read the Bible to better understand God's character and action. I read ancient histories and secondary sources, accounts of the crucifixion and resurrection. I read books about where the Bible came from and why I should take it seriously.

This process takes months, maybe a year. Saying how I feel out loud, turning my anger toward God and voicing it consistently, this throws me into an argument with God, the best kind of argument, the kind that leads to realization and peace and ultimately connection.

When all is said and done, I am convinced Jesus came to earth, died, and was raised. I'm convinced the Bible is a holy book. I'm convinced God exists and that God is ultimately the standard for what's truly good. Faith upon faith falls into place like Tetris shapes.

This process seems clean and easy typed up into paragraphs printed in a book published years after the fact, the fog of doubt burned off. But it wasn't easy. The last thing I wanted to do, mired in grief, was to start a fight with God. It was exhausting and emotional and life-upturning. In that season of uncertainty and seeking, I wondered who I was if God wasn't. A financially dependent preacher's wife considering a life in ministry, I had a lot invested in faith. For a while, I was on the verge of going bankrupt in every way, and I felt those high stakes in my bones. But looking back, I see this burning down and rebuilding of my faith as maybe the best thing that came of my grief, which is saying more than might be expected, because this grief ends up shaping me in ways for which I will forever be thankful.

Side note: If you find your grief burning down your house, this little story of mine won't be enough to shore up your faith. That's not the point. I want you to know that your faith can survive this but only if you turn your anger toward God instead of away, and only if you're willing to show up to the fight.

~~~

What did I think God owed me? I think, in the end, I thought He owed me the answer I wanted to the prayer I prayed in that moment before I knew for sure my brother'd died.

Did He owe me that? Maybe not. But that was hard to reconcile with passages like Matthew 21:22, "If you believe, you will receive whatever you ask for in prayer," or James 5:16, "The prayer of a righteous person is powerful and effective."

I thought, however irrationally, that God owed me what I'd asked for.

Recently, I thought again of this prayer and this frustrating anger I couldn't quite wrap up and put away. As I turned it over and over in my mind, I found myself struck by something I hadn't noticed before. I pulled out my journal and flipped through the pages looking for the exact words I'd used that December morning. I found them and almost fell out of my seat. Tears streaming down my cheeks, I read, "God, You love me like You loved Mary and Martha. Raise my brother like You did theirs."

I grabbed my Bible and turned to John 11, running my fingers down the page, looking. I found Martha's words in verse 21: "'Lord,' Martha said to Jesus, 'if You had been here, my brother would not have died.'" I realized in this moment that Martha and Mary felt the exact same way I did: angry,
~~~

owed. I realized their brother's resurrection didn't come when they wanted it, either. I realized I am right to feel like something's been stolen from me. I am right to feel like God owes me. I'm right because, like Martha, I've been promised abundant, eternal life. I've been promised resurrection.

But I'm wrong to think God has decided not to give it, wrong to think He's reneged on His promise. Jesus says to Martha, "Your brother will rise again." And I know, deep down, God's saying it to me.

So that's it? The anger's gone?

No.

It was good to let go of my anger toward God. He didn't deserve it. I am, however, still angry. I figure I always will be. I'm angry like Jesus was angry standing in front of Lazarus's tomb.

A few years ago, my husband Justin preached on John 11. When he got to verse 33, he slowed down and zoomed in. It reads: "When Jesus saw her weeping, and the Jews who had come along with her also weeping, He was deeply moved in spirit and troubled." I thought it lovely to see Jesus moved, to see compassion in His eyes. But Justin went a different way than I'd expected. He said that phrase "deeply moved in spirit and troubled" doesn't indicate sorrow at all. He said, actually, Jesus is angry.

I tracked down the phrase myself and found this:

> The original meaning of the word [translated "deeply moved"] is 'to snort, as of horses.' Passing to the moral sense, it expresses disturbance of the mind—vehement agitation. This may express itself in sharp admonition, in words of anger against a person, or

in a physical shudder, answering to the intensity of the emotion. (Ellicott's Commentary for English Readers)

The *Cambridge Bible for Schools and Colleges* says this: "In all cases, as in classical Greek and in the LXX., it expresses not sorrow but indignation or severity. It means (1) literally, of animals, 'to snort, growl;' then metaphorically (2) 'to be very angry or indignant;' (3) 'to command sternly, under threat of displeasure.'"

So, on the road to see His dead friend, watching His dead friend's sister weeping at His feet, Jesus feels angry. And in His anger, Jesus says, "Where have you laid him?" Is it possible that the resurrection of Lazarus, the very miracle that will ultimately get Jesus killed, is an act of indignation, a refusal to let death win even just a little bit?

We Christians, the people called to love our enemies, the ones held to a standard of compassion and forgiveness, will find, if we look close enough, one giant loophole, one place where anger finds its holy fruition. We, the Living, are permitted a true enemy. That enemy, "the last enemy to be destroyed," is Death. (I Corinthians 15:26) Jesus is infuriated by Death. God is, too. Remember the scene He makes at the cross, spewing darkness, breaking the ground, spitting up corpses?

Jesus says, "I am the resurrection and the life." (John 11:25) His very identity stands in opposition to Death. And when we choose Him we choose Life, and in choosing Life we take up arms against the enemy, Death.

I didn't understand this fully when I died in the baptistery and rose to new life at nine years old. I began to understand it more when I buried my brother and began a vigil, waiting for the day when he'd rise to new life again.

In his book *Tribe*, Sebastian Junger argues that war provides a sense of "social solidarity," that a shared enemy is one of the most powerful ways to bind a people. He asks a combat vet whether he'd rather have a close friend or an enemy, and the vet says *enemy*. He says he has plenty of friends. The idea is that people grow close in their combined efforts to defend against something. When people have no outside force to oppose, they turn inside and begin opposing one another.

I think Christians need an enemy. Might I propose Death? Let's get angry at Death together. Let's fight Death together.

What does Jesus do when Death makes Him angry? He responds with resurrection. He overturns Death's work. Whenever I get to missing my brother, whenever I get to feeling robbed, I center my anger on Death and ask myself, "What can I do to wage war against Death today? How can I steal back some of what I'm owed?"

The only response that makes sense is to live. To really, fully, abundantly live. And to welcome other people into that Life. To build bridges leading to Life. To preach Life and teach Life and write about Life. To be like Christ, who contained Life, whose "life was the light of all mankind." (John 1:4)

A few years ago, on the anniversary of Bobby's death, I sat down to make a list of "Ways to Fight Death Today." I wrote things like these:

Take the girls to a nursing home. Bring homemade cards
Write a blog post about light and hope
Have a family water balloon fight
Sing
Cuddle
Forgive a friend
Make an extravagant meal

I made the list because, as usual, I was angry, missing my brother's laugh, his loyalty, his jokes, the way he made me feel like the smartest person in the room. I wanted him back (I always do). And so, like a comic book hero, I plotted my holy revenge, and took aim at my enemy.

JANUARY 16, 2003

I miss Bobby so bad. Any time something happens that makes me just the smallest bit angry I break down. It's like I can't feel emotion without losing it completely. When I get really happy. When I get really angry, sad, frustrated, confused—whatever. I can't function without thinking of him and getting sick. I get this feeling in my stomach. It's a feeling I've never felt before. It's despair. It's a hole. It's a rock tied to my soul that's pulling me further and further into the depths...

Yes, it's like drowning, but it's more than that. It's like a darkness that's slowly enveloping you except you don't want to fight the darkness. It feels warm and when you've been in the dark for long enough you don't care about the light. You don't care if you ever see it again. You just want to forget. You don't notice that there aren't any people around. You don't care. You don't care about anything. The only light in your world is the dim glow of paid advertising on your 10-inch TV.

I got a job today. Mom said that Bobby would be proud. I guess he would have been...

CHAPTER 7

HAUNTED

"Numbing the pain for a while will make it worse when you finally feel it."

J.K. Rowling, *Harry Potter and the Goblet of Fire*

When I get back home from all the traveling to Florida and New York, not home exactly but where I live anyway, Alabama with its red clay and cotton and indiscernible accents, I start looking for a job. Because I don't have one and because I can't sit around all day crying, eating pizza from the gas station down the street, and watching *Gilmore Girls* seasons on DVD. Even at 21, I have a sense that this isn't healthy grieving.

How exactly I pull myself together, create a resume, and interview for a job, I have no idea. This is one of those lift-a-car moments. My mom tells me it's important, a job will distract me from the hurt. My husband says, "You need *something*."

Armed with a BA in English from a school no one's heard of and only one category of recent job experience, I plan exploratory trips to the two small newspapers within 30 minutes of my house. I pull into the first to find two sisters putting out a once-a-week community newsletter, not at all in need of staff. They say, "Go to Athens, and see Sonny," and so I do. I ask if they're hiring at the desk, and within two minutes I'm seated across from the editor, watching him grimace at my resume. He hires me on the spot, and I start the next day.

My first day on the job I write an article about a beauty pageant winner and cry in my car in the McDonald's parking lot during lunch.

My life looks like a Dali painting, all melting clocks and elephants on stilts, surreal.

On day two, about an hour before I'm scheduled to go home, my editor comes to my desk with a story. He says, "Accident out on the highway." (We have only one highway here.) He says the car's totaled. Police at the scene. Kid killed.

My heart starts racing, my hands get hot, my vision blurs.

"I need you to run out there and get a picture. And call the parents to try to get a quote."

I don't move.

"You okay?" he asks.

I don't speak.

"Let me get you the location," he says. Other reporters, editors, the part-time photographer have gathered around my desk to hear the news. They're trying to figure out if they know the kid. A fatality is big news at a little paper. The office is buzzing.

Tears crammed into pools in the corners of my eyes, I say too quietly to the gathered crowd, "Can someone else do it?"

I don't know these people assembled at my desk, and they know nothing about me. For almost two days I have enjoyed this anonymity, sitting in a room with strangers who treat me just the same as they would anyone else, strangers who don't know what's happened. These people have expectations of me. They bump me in the hall. They ignore me in the breakroom when I seem sad. They expect me to be hardy and don't look at me like I might break at any moment. I like that about this new place, this office full of people who don't know I'm Jennifer whose brother has died. *But that's about to be over.*

I say to the faces now facing mine, "My brother just died in a car accident."

Every set of eyes rounds and drops. My editor says, "Of course." My associate editor says, "I've got it." The photographer says, "I can stay late and grab the picture." And they all move away from my undecorated desk and from me, the new girl nobody knows, while I try not to explode and make a bigger mess.

Forty-five minutes later I sneak away to my car and cry so hard I can't see straight and have to call my husband to tell him I won't be coming home tonight because I can't stop crying long enough to see the road in front of me. He offers to drive the thirty minutes and pick me up. Instead I drive in bursts. Five minutes, stop to cry for ten. Five minutes more, pull over in a field…

You can't run away from death. You can't bury it in a hole or shove it in a big marble wall and walk away and expect it to stay there. Death is everywhere. It's in a play in New York and on the highway in Athens, Alabama. And even if you found a place where death didn't live, you'd bring it with you. Death's perfume gets in your clothes.

Sometimes, though, you forget about death for a minute, and you start living a kind of normal-ish life, sending emails and interviewing beauty pageant queens and filling out tax paperwork. Those moments of forgetting would be lovely if you could realize you were in one when you were. Instead, we only realize we've achieved that kind of beautiful distraction when, out of nowhere, death swoops in and punches us in the gut, pulling us back into our new, terrible normal.

Death found me in the grocery store, in traffic, in church, in the drive-thru line, on the couch watching TV, and in the newsroom of a little Alabama newspaper. It was like life was a haunted house with spooks jumping out from behind every corner.

That is exactly how life after my brother died felt—haunted.

I go to a fundraiser for a scholarship fund in Bobby's honor, and I see him across the room. Bobby. I see Bobby.

I shake my head, close my eyes, open them, and realize this is Bobby's middle school friend, Justin, who looks remarkably like my brother. Once, my dad went to pick up Bobby after a chorus concert and put his hand on Justin's shoulder by accident. Their teachers sometimes confused them—both tall, both blonde, both slim, both usually smiling. I would like to avoid this young man who looks too much like my brother, but my mom calls me over and after an awkward reintroduction I lose my mind and ask if I can see his hands. I hold them. *People will let crazy, grieving people do all manner of strange things.* It is nothing like holding Bobby's hands.

I will be sick over this moment for years. This feeling of holding someone else's hands sticks in my skull and slays me.

ccc

For a while I cannot eat Eggo waffles. The memories of making them with Bobby, of the exact toaster, butter, microwave, syrup process we'd perfected is too much. I avoid the frozen breakfast foods aisle at the grocery store. Eating at Chick-fil-A is entirely off the table. Chili's, too. Too much history.

My house reminds me of him, and I want to move. The pictures and lights he helped to hang taunt me, and the couch he slept on at Mom's 40th birthday party.

Sports remind me of him. All sports. I can't watch any sort of athletic event without remembering the time he tried it, the time we played it, the game we attended, the signs we made for the game on TV, the equipment he bought and never used. Every player brings memories of Bobby's high school scouting reports sent via voicemail—*You should see this kid Lebron James play ball.*

Shows on TV. Stores at the mall. My clothes...

Sometimes a word, a word people don't use every day, will snap my attention back to the time Bobby used it to make me laugh.

With Bobby just barely out of the world, like he's stepped outside for a minute, everything still smells of his cologne. The memory of him is unavoidable and wrecking. There is no getting on or forgetting or distraction. Every next minute carries a dozen inciting incidents.

These incidents, these accidental brushes with the ghost of my brother, hurt. Every one is a kick or stab, a knocking-loose of the wind in my lungs. I don't feel safe in a Bobby-haunted world.

And so I hide.

I eat lunch in my car to avoid the breakroom and whatever awkward thing someone might say. I limit what I eat and where I go and what I watch and what I wear and what I read and what I listen to. I camp out on my couch and in my bed and don't answer phone calls. When I do hang out with people, I seek out new friends, friends who easily forget I'm grieving.

Sometimes I try denial, pretending nothing's wrong and I'm not actually hurting and I'm fine. Don't worry about it; I'm fine. I don't need help; I'm fine. That movie didn't make me cry; I have allergies. I'M FINE.

I also self-medicate. In search of that lovely thing called numbness, I eat. A lot. I eat pizza and ice cream and pumpkin muffins and Reese's Cups. I eat bags of Reese's Cups. The little black paper cups litter my carpet like confetti. I don't drink alcohol for two reasons: (1) I haven't tried it yet and don't know anything of its magical powers, and (2) I think I'll go to Hell if I do.

My fourth ghost-busting tool: overwork. I wake up, throw on clothes, drive to work, and stay there until eight or nine at night. On the weekends I devote myself to teaching Bible class and visiting sick people and reading test-prep books for the GRE. I write articles for magazines and help my husband figure out how to help our little church. I build a wall of work to protect me from the memories, painful and poking.

I don't like haunted houses. I hate them. I hate surprises. I hate being scared. I despise being knocked off-balance by the unexpected. I don't want that kind of pain. And so I stay out of haunted houses. But grief doesn't work like that. It's not contained to some place you avoid. The events around you aren't what's causing the pain. The pain is inside you. You carry it with you everywhere, and no matter how hard you try to avoid it, stuff it, distract yourself from it, numb it, or deny it, it will find you.

The night before the morning my brother died I had dinner guests. I was 21 and playing house. I made lasagna with Ragu spaghetti sauce and cheese from a bag. Justin pulled down the board games we'd received as wedding presents from the closet.

Bobby called during dinner, and we let the call go to the answering machine. He left a message. He said my name.

After dinner and games, our friends went home, and I went to sleep, forgetting to return my brother's call, tired. Later, past midnight, he'd call again, and Justin would pick up. I'd wave off the phone, half asleep. Justin would spend a half hour talking to Bobby that night, helping keep his mind awake as he drove. Bobby told him about a girl he'd been dating, said maybe she was the one. He read a note she'd written him. We'd find it in his wallet later, when the coroner gave us his things.

Justin was one of the last people to ever talk to Bobby. A blessing. I was the person who chose against it. A curse.

I would think about this choice every day for a year, often sitting on my side of the bed, pushing the answering machine button one more time to hear him say my name.

What if I'd answered the phone? What if I'd noticed how tired he was and convinced him to pull over? What if I'd offered to pay for a hotel?

Maybe things would be different…

Even if I hadn't intervened, what if I'd talked to him? What if I had one more conversation to recall? What if I'd been able to tell him I loved him, as I always did when we talked? What if I'd been able to hear him say he loved me, as he always did before we hung up?

Would this have been easier? Even a little?

I carried this guilt around for months. I didn't tell anyone about the call; I just stuffed the pain down deep and tried not to feel it. I mostly failed.

One night, a year or so after Bobby died, I was talking to my mom on the phone. Our conversations had been strained ever since our trip to New York. We weren't good on the phone. We never had been. We struggled to ask good questions. We struggled to think anything mattered enough to talk about it. We were both sad, both a little angry at the other person for not helping us feel less sad. Every phone call, intended for connection, left us feeling further and further apart. It didn't make sense, but it's how things went. Death messes everything up.

This night I was feeling that distance, feeling like I wasn't telling her everything, like I was hiding parts of myself, like I wasn't giving her a chance to love me. And so I told her about the call from Bobby, about how I'd ignored it and how relentlessly guilty and sad that made me. I don't cry in front of my mom much. She doesn't cry much in front of me. But I did cry that night. I cried and I told the truth and it felt right and good.

Just saying it out loud, admitting what I'd done and owning the way I felt about it released something inside me; it was like a valve turned and the pressure that had built up and threatened explosion suddenly lessened. Finally, I could breathe.

My mom grabbed my words like a baton, eager to love me. She told me not to feel guilty. *How could you have known? Your brother loved you. You were an amazing sister.* Her response reminded me that it was safe to share my pain with people who love me.

Days later, I was still feeling lighter, freer, like a brick had been lifted off my chest.

I'd decide to tell my ladies' Bible class about my struggle to get out of the house. I'd tell them why I was working so much and how tired I was. I'd also tell them more about Bobby. About why I missed him so much.

One confession, one bucket of truth pulled up from the well, would lead to more and more buckets, more and more courage to talk about Bobby, and then courage to go places he went and eat food he loved and watch sports without fear. If I cried, I'd tell the people at my table about my brother and how much he liked the team playing football on the TV screen or how much he loved the chicken tenders here; maybe I'd even keep going and tell them about his chicken tender ranking system. I began to see these encounters with memories of Bobby not as disasters to be avoided but as opportunities, opportunities to remember the brother I loved and to connect more deeply with my friends and family.

Sometimes my tears made people uncomfortable. Sometimes friends tried to derail a story of mine with their apologies, thinking I didn't really want to tell it. But I did want to tell it, and I often would anyway, even when people seemed uncomfortable. I decided that the only way to deal with these memories and the only way to deal with this pain was to talk about it.

Eventually, Justin would accidentally delete Bobby's message on the machine, and I would lose the last recording I had of Bobby's voice. I would cry for days. I cried rivers spilling into pools, flooding my house with sadness and regret. I would miss Bobby's voice. But fortunately, I still had memories, memories to embrace and share, stories to tell, places to go and remember.

I am tempted to look back at Jennifer, a girl in her early twenties, freshly married and bereaved, and judge her for all the time she spent crying in her bed, judge her for the melodramatic journal entries and self-pity-ridden prayers. But the truth is that those tears sowed healing, that the Jennifer who writes these words today, mostly whole and well, exists because that Jennifer was willing to confront her pain, was willing to deal with her guilt and sadness and anger and abandonment. Because at some point she said, *I am not going to hide anymore. I'm going to feel these things I'm feeling. I'm going to talk to people. I'm going to pray. And I'm not going to pretend like nothing's wrong.*

One night in my graduate Shakespeare class, about a year after Bobby had died, six months after I'd quit the newspaper and gone back to school, I told my classmates about my brother's death. We were studying *Romeo and Juliet* and talking about how this was a complicated text to teach to teens, about how death could be romanticized, about how that's not at all what Shakespeare was trying to do.

I piped up and said, "We can be tempted to only notice the lovers and miss all the people around them who'll carry the shrapnel of death deep inside themselves—parents, friends, even bystanders." I said that when my brother died, hundreds of people grieved, all of them diminished by his death. I pointed to the prince's last few words. Mediator of the violence and hatred that soak the play, the prince stands in the presence of the two dead, too-young bodies, and says these words to their grieving families: "All are punish'd."

As I spoke—the youngest person in my class and yet the only one who'd ever suffered the loss of a young loved one—

the room went silent. Heads leaned in. Eyes locked on mine. It was as if I carried a magical wisdom.

Later, friends would ask, "How did you do that? How were you able to share like that without completely losing it?"

I think I could because I had before. Because I'd learned through experience that grief expressed is better than grief hidden. It's better for me and better for the people around me, too. People get to know the real me. People are given an opportunity to see me and love me and help me. And sometimes, as in this case, those people find their own blessing in the story, they're made stronger and wiser by my experience.

The prince in *Romeo and Juliet* ends the play with words you may well know. He says,

Go hence, to have more talk of these sad things;
Some shall be pardon'd, and some punished:
For never was a story of more woe
Than this of Juliet and her Romeo.

I remembered those last two lines, but today, looking back over the play to cite it here, I realized I hadn't noticed the first. Rather than telling the grieving families to go hence and have "no more talk of these sad things," he tells them *to* talk of these sad things. It's as if Shakespeare steps in to say that the way forward in grief is to talk about sad things, even the stories with the most woe—to parse them and seek understanding in them. *That makes sense, given Shakespeare's proclivity for tragedy.*

It makes sense to me, too, because speaking about my sadness has been the only way to handle it. Instead of waiting for the ghost of my brother to jump out from around the corner, I welcome him into the room. I carry his story in front of me in open hands. I tell stories about him to friends. I say to my girls, "That is such an Uncle Bobby thing to do." I eat wherever I like, Chili's or Chick-fil-A, and say to myself, "Bobby would have loved this." I watch a great football game and think, "What a joy it was to watch football with him."

Instead of avoiding the ghosts, I've learned to turn on the lights. I welcome the memory of my brother into my life and even the pain that tags along behind. Slowly the pain becomes less and slowly the joy grows greater.

CHAPTER 8

VERY, VERY SAD

"'Now look what's happened,' I thought. 'I've seen a bird. I've seen a flycatcher, when all the birds in the world should be dead.'"

Sonali Deraniyagala, *Wave*

One day in October, the October before Bobby died, just a couple months after Justin and I moved into our new house, Bobby drove down from school to spend the weekend with us. We, of course, put him to work. I have this picture I love of Justin standing on a chair to install a light and Bobby standing on the ground, hugging Justin around the waist "to keep him steady."

This weekend was particularly hot for October, poor conditions for our big project: putting in a mailbox. In theory, it should have been easy. Dig a hole. Drop the wooden post in the hole. Close up the hole. But in practice, not so much. The problem was the clay. All three of us had grown up in Florida with sand for soil, and this Alabama red clay was nothing like that. It baked in the summer heat and digging it up was an all-day task. I remember watching Justin and Bobby drinking water by the gallon as they took turns trying to crack the ceramic earth. Eventually, perhaps when a glass of water spilled, we remembered the powerful properties of liquid, and made mud and headway. When Bobby left for school on Sunday after church, he backed down our driveway past our well-planted mailbox. It was the last time he'd visit my home.

With Bobby dead, the mailbox becomes an altar, a reminder that my brother lived, visited my house, and loved me enough to sweat through his shirt so I'd have a place to receive mail. I love my mailbox.

It's after lunch and I'm doing dishes when I hear the truck backing up—a giant semi trying to fit in my neighbor's not-so-giant driveway. First comes the beeping. Then comes the thud. It's Justin who opens the front door just in time to see the truck pull away, right past what is left of our mailbox. I don't know what's happened until he calls my name. I go to the door to see my altar cracked in half.

I feel as if this truck has run over my family dog. No, I feel as if this truck has killed my brother.

This happens about six months after Bobby died, and it is a picture of everything I'm feeling. Mostly that, despite my best efforts to hang on, Bobby is (and all my memories of him are) slipping from my fingers. I lie in bed trying to see specific moments with him and already I struggle to make out his face or hear his voice. I misplace his ring and search the whole house for a week and can't find it. My parents stop paying his phone bill and the voicemail message disappears.

I'm losing him.

I read Elizabeth Bishop's poem *One Art*, and I weep. Losing is the easiest hardest thing to master.

I walk to the end of the drive and sit beside the wreckage, trying to imagine a way to repair what is so obviously irreparable. I want to call Bobby, to make him come back and help me again, to dig up more clay and plant a mailbox again. But I can't. And it's not because he's out of town. It's not because he's off at college. It's because he's dead. He can't come help me, and he won't ever come help me again, and it is in this moment that I realize in a way I haven't yet that Bobby is never coming back.

The pain of this loss, the practical consequences of his absence, the growing separation between us, the days like bricks in a widening wall, this tower of evidence that he's gone—this pain is the worst pain yet. It's worse because it's certain and feels permanent. This is no dream. I'm not waking up.

Crying and sleeping become the primary stages of my life cycle.

This is the part of grief that people on the outside expect—the tears, mostly. But when you live this part, the tears come as a shock. You wonder how you could cry so much and so often. You wonder how you are making so much liquid; surely this is a physical impossibility. I read in a book once about a woman whose tears flooded her house and then her country. This seemed reasonable to me. I could flood Alabama, at least.

Joan Didion said, in her book about losing her husband, "I wanted to get the tears out of the way so I could act sensibly." That's because tears hold you hostage. You don't want to leave your house because you might cry in the grocery store and make a scene. You avoid meaningful conversations. You try not to read sad books or watch sad movies. And just when you think you're safe, the tears surprise you at your desk at work or on the subway on your way home and you remember you're at their mercy.

I have a friend ask me why she isn't feeling better yet. "It's been a year," she says. "Why do I still feel so bad?" I tell her, "Actually, the second year was my worst." I don't know if this is true for everyone, but friends tell me it's true for them. Maybe it's more accurate to say months 6 to 18 are the worst. Maybe it's stupid to assess the worst season of your life and pinpoint the worst of the worst moments. But maybe it helps, when you're 12 months into grieving, to know that very few people feel better at this point, and a lot of people feel worse.

Here's why so many of us feel so bad after so many months:

1. We have come to terms with the reality and permanence of our loss. We can't close our eyes and pretend anymore. This is real.

2. People are treating us like normal humans again. They've forgotten why we're so sad. In fact, our sadness and incapacitation are becoming stressful for them. They need us to get our stuff together, clean the house, respond to emails on time, pay our taxes, and brush our teeth. Probably we hate them for this and decide to live alone. But alone doesn't pay the bills and alone means no help and alone feels lonely.

3. We are waist-deep in some pretty crappy habits. We're likely overweight, drunk, TV-dependent, or addicted to porn. And those crappy habits have crappy consequences, like making us feel bad about ourselves (or *for* ourselves) All. The. Time.

4. Things changed when our person died. Maybe we had to move. Maybe we changed jobs. Maybe we lost friends. Almost certainly we had to say goodbye to one way of

living and adapt to another. We have not adapted to our new life yet. We're still on the far side of the hump.

I don't realize these things at month six or month eight. I think something is wrong. I think surely I am broken—I shouldn't still be this sad. I start wondering if I will ever not be sad.

C.S. Lewis wrote after losing his wife,

> I once read the sentence "I lay awake all night with a toothache, thinking about the toothache and about lying awake." That's true to life. Part of every misery is, so to speak, the misery's shadow or reflection: the fact that you don't merely suffer but have to keep on thinking about the fact that you suffer. I not only live each endless day in grief, but live each day thinking about living each day in grief.

This is exactly it: You are sad, you are sad that you are still sad, and you are sad that you might be sad forever.

Sometimes I feel happy. This is strange and might be good, except it makes me nervous, the way people around me are so glad I'm smiling. I worry they will decide I'm happy now, that the grief has passed. I pretend to not be happy so people will keep letting me make excuses. I am terrified someone will take away my sad pass.

Didion wrote about her dead husband, "A single person is missing for you, and the whole world is empty." My life isn't empty without my brother. I'm married, employed, still a daughter and friend, still talented and driven, still purposed by God. But somehow Bobby's dying makes my life *seem* empty. Maybe Bobby's dying opened my eyes like the Ecclesiastes writer had his opened. Bobby's dying leaves me saying, "Vanity, vanity, everything is vanity." (1:2)

After Bobby dies, I am plagued by the unpredictability of life and death. I keep wondering why I should devote so much effort to living here when death might come tomorrow and prove all my effort senseless. I have never been so certain of my own smallness, the mist-nature of my life. I ask no one in particular, "If death is our destiny, what does it matter *when* we die? Why not turn ourselves over to it now? Why keep fighting?"

I can't remember the first time I imagine killing myself. Likely it is in the first year after loss. Likely I think about driving off an overpass, plowing through the guardrails and soaring through the sky like Thelma and Louise. I doubt cars soar like that as they fall off overpasses. Probably they flip and drop. *Quickly.* That is if it's even possible to get up enough speed to make it past the guardrails. When I have this thought, I tell myself it's not possible.

I have this thought too often.

It starts with overpasses, but later I will imagine slit wrists and bathtubs or drowning like Virginia Woolf with rocks in my pockets. *I find peace in my excellent swimming skills and my suspicion that drowning would never work.*

These are not active thoughts, these visions of death. They creep from the corners in quiet moments. I do not choose these thoughts, but they unfold in such lovely detail, blood like watercolor-red on porcelain, water like pure, perfect peace.

It isn't that I want to die. I don't. But living has become so hard. Every part of it. I spend more and more time in bed wishing I didn't have to wake up.

I go to my doctor because my mom says I should, because she and Dad have both been on medication and it's helping, and I need help. I make an appointment, show up, get myself out of the car, and tell my doctor I think maybe I am depressed. I tell her I am sad, that my brother died and since then I've been buried in sadness, that the sadness is getting in the way of me living my life. That even when I'm not sad I feel heavy. That everything is harder than it seems like it should be.

This amount of sustained effort—getting to the doctor and spilling my guts—requires Herculean strength. It is no doubt supernaturally deployed.

My doctor smiles kindly as I speak and writes a prescription. She tells me I have situational depression and to take the pills according to the directions. She says, "These are going to even out your mood." She is nice and not such a good listener.

I will realize later that she doesn't ask many questions, that she never asks if I was depressed before my brother died, that she doesn't ask about my (rather extensive) family history of mental illness, that she doesn't ask about my support system or what I'm eating. She doesn't recommend counseling. I'm not thinking of this when I leave the office. I have gone to the doctor and she has given me this bottle of pills and I am feeling like finally I will be able to breathe.

Two things they don't tell you when you pick up your magic happy pills at the pharmacy:

1. Because you are depressed, you are probably going to do a terrible job taking these pills according to the directions. You will sleep past the time each day you should take them. You will forget to eat or drink water. You will forget whether or not you already took one. You will also hem and haw over whether or not they're working and sometimes use the lack of

"results" to justify not taking them.

2. These pills, when you buckle down and get help taking them on the regular, will make you feel less bad, but they might also make you feel less. And for you (for me), that is actually the biggest problem—the numbness.

After a month I throw the bottle of leftover pills in the trashcan at the mall and refuse to go back to the doctor. This is not good advice. *Don't follow my example.*

In a letter to Jonas Von Stockhausen in 1532, Martin Luther advises his friend on how to deal with melancholy. He writes, "Good friends have informed me that the evil one is tempting you severely with weariness of life and longing for death." Luther, all out of tenderness but full of faith, litters the page with exclamation marks encouraging Von Stockhausen to rebuke the forces of the devil so clearly at work: "You must be resolute… and say to yourself wrathfully, 'No matter how unwilling you are to live, you are going to live and like it! This is what God wants… Begone you thoughts of the devil! To hell with dying and death!'"

Sometimes I wish I had a friend like this, so blunt and assertive. *You're going to live and like it, Gerhardt! To hell with death and dying!* (Can we all agree that "to hell with death and dying" would make a terrific tattoo?)

I get that not everyone feels suicidal after the death of a loved one. Personally, I'm sure grief triggered something chemical and latent in me, something I already struggled to suppress but finally couldn't hold in. But even if you don't struggle with the impulse to die, you probably find yourself tempted to be less and less alive. We mourners get out of bed later and fall into bed earlier. We stay in more. We go out less. We talk to fewer and fewer people. Maybe we eat less. Maybe we eat more but stop paying attention to the taste. We take fewer showers and fewer risks.

In grief, it's common to shrink, common to yearn like a bear in winter for a dark cave and a long sleep. This is not all bad; hibernation may enable a strong spring. But if we stay in the cave, we'll let death win.

Now is about the time in the book when I begin quoting the young adult novel *The Hunger Games*. It's relevant, I promise.

If you haven't read *The Hunger Games* trilogy, it's about a messed up world in which children are required to fight to the death in an annual event called the Hunger Games. It features Katniss Everdeen, a young woman with extraordinary archery skills and surprising kindness, and the young man Peeta Mellark, who is even more kind and courageous and, of course, in love with her. Both have been chosen to compete in the games, and both have been assigned an incompetent mentor whose drunken advice is "stay alive." *Obviously*. Later, though, Peeta will dwell on those words, finding in them more wisdom than he caught at first. He wonders if it's possible to stay himself, to stay alive, even as he dies.

Those words have stuck with me, too. For years, I had them written on a chalkboard in my bedroom: "Stay alive." For my birthday, my sister-in-law had bracelets made with the words stamped into them. I wear them almost every day.

For the grieving, "stay alive" is some of the best advice you'll hear.

Our instinct is to respond to death with death. To stop seeing. To stop exploring. To stop doing. Stop feeling. Stop wondering. Stop dreaming. Stop wanting. Stop connecting.

Stop loving.

How do we stay alive when death is close and despair pulls? Perhaps we say to ourselves what Luther said we should: "You are going to live and like it!" Perhaps we fight the temptation to live less by choosing to live more.

Stay alive means when death takes your loved one, love harder, deeper, wider.

Stay alive means when death brings despair, don't give in. Get up. Take a shower. Make your bed. Do one hard thing.

Stay alive means when death makes you feel like you've already given in and may as well give in some more, have grace for your failures and courage to try again.

Stay alive means when death has you covering the brakes, scared, living small, you choose adventure and holy risk, refusing to let death draw the boundary lines of your life.

Stay alive means when death gives you a storehouse of excuses, reasons to say "no thanks" or "I can't," you embrace the gift of community and go.

When death tries to draw you into darkness, you stay alive in Christ, refusing to walk in sin, even when it's hard to muster self-control, even when you'd rather dull your senses with reckless excess.

Stay alive means drinking from the water of life and eating from the tree of life and sharing the bread of life. It means receiving what Jesus offers when He promises, "I have come that they may have life, and have it to the full." (John 10:10)

When death draws you into isolation and separation, it is a holy act of rebellion to pick up the phone and call your mother.

To go to a party.

To forgive a friend.

To believe the best about something stupid someone said.

If death is separation, life is love. Seek it out.

When death sows doubt, it is a holy act of defiance to read the Psalms aloud.

To sing along to worship songs on the radio in the car, one hand raised, one on the wheel.

To take communion, to eat the body and drink the blood, taking into yourself the life that defeated death.

To proclaim through tears, fist raised to Heaven, *I hate this! But I trust You.*

If death is doubt, life is faith. Hold onto it.

When death stands in your way, like a dropped curtain at the end of a play, and makes you think maybe everything good is behind you, it is a holy act of defiance to make lunch plans for tomorrow.

To make a new friend.

To invest yourself in a hard-to-solve problem.

To dream a new dream.

To imagine a new Heaven, new earth, and new you.

If Death says you only have the past, Life walks boldly into the future, building and forging what's next with the unshakable hope that what's to come is better than what's been.

All of these things—love, faith, and hope—are the battle cry of the Kingdom of Life. If you want to stay alive in the face of Death, these are the things you pursue. And if you pursue them, not only do the thoughts of death and despair dissipate, *slowly*, so does the constant and heavy sadness. Soon, you will feel the first blush of joy.

I didn't feel like pursuing love, faith, and hope when my brother died, but luckily it wasn't entirely up to me. The Spirit of God can't stop growing those things in His people, and even in my despair, I'd hear the Spirit calling me. I heard Him in the people around me—people inviting me to lunch, people encouraging me to write, people welcoming me into friendship. I heard Him in the Word—promising me a future, telling me stories of His faithfulness and love. And I heard Him in prayer where my groans and yearnings turned into action steps.

God called me to life. And slowly, though I often didn't want to at all, I began answering.

I don't know when the despair lifted. Maybe it was the day I decided to rollerblade from my house to the church building five miles away, over hills and through fields, on two-lane highways with cars taking turns too fast. I skated and sweated and felt the rush of wind through my hair. Every time I rode past the house of one of the old ladies from church, my husband would receive a phone call telling him to come get me. This thing I was doing (*rollerblading?*) was evidently ridiculous and dangerous. Justin would say, "She's exercising. It's good for her," and the old ladies would guffaw. I'd make it to the church building out of breath and smelling terrible, but feeling very much alive.

Maybe I started to feel better during that first Vacation Bible School, when I was writing all the curriculum for every Bible class, including the adults, plus writing and directing skits and making sets and painting signs for the front yard. Maybe the flurry of activity and purpose pulled me out and drew me in.

Maybe it was playing cards—our new neighbors, friends, calling twice a week to see if we were up for Spades. I almost never wanted to play, because I almost never wanted to leave my house. But they could see the light on in our living room and knew we were home and I had no excuses, so off we went to play cards and eat chili dogs. Though I almost never wanted to play, every game led me further out of my cave. We'd play for four hours, learning the game, learning each other, and laughing.

I can remember plenty of joys in those dark days, joys like stars: no-stakes poker tournaments in the church basement, teaching the elementary Bible class, painting lessons at the art museum, good books, lively discussions with like-minded and not-like-minded classmates, a trip to California with my parents, a new puppy.

All of these things together, like cords in a rope, helped lead me out of the dark.

At first this joy, the joy that comes from living, will fit like your father's coat. You will wear it poorly. It will itch. You will want to take it off. *And you can sometimes if you need to.* But you will also need to keep putting it on. Keep trying to reach out, to connect, to believe, to hope. To live.

CHAPTER 9

AFRAID

"It's all very well to read about sorrows and imagine yourself living through them heroically, but it's not so nice when you really come to have them, is it?"

L.M. Montgomery, *Anne of Green Gables*

It's late. I'm in a computer lab on the bottom floor of the building where I work. The job is "research assistant." I record lectures for online coursework, but now, looking back, I can't remember a single co-worker's name or face. I can't remember my boss or what my desk looked like. Again with the memory-smudging.

This room, the computer lab—which I do remember clearly—is crowded with mostly quiet college students staring at glowing screens. I'm in the back trying to stare at a screen, too, my legs folded up beneath me as I perch on the very corner of my chair. I'm biting my nails, but I don't know that. I never do until I've bitten them too far. I've been off work for 30 minutes, waiting that whole time in this computer lab for my husband, who is very late to pick me up and not answering my texts.

He's not answering my texts because, of course, he is dead.

I don't know that, but how could it not be true? My throat constricts. My hands shake. Every muscle is tense. Every time the doorknob turns and the door pushes open I expect not my husband, but a policeman. "Mrs. Gerhardt?" he'll say. Maybe he'll whisper to the lab monitor first. Check the log for my name. I think about it longer and realize there's no way for the police to know I'm here. Likely they'll go looking for me at home. I expect there's a policeman at my door right now. I think maybe my neighbor will know where to direct him. I wonder if she'll call to tell me he's coming.

All I can do is wait for the policeman who, I suppose, will find me somehow. I'll need him to give me a ride home.

To pass the time, I Google, "How much does a funeral cost?"

Fifteen minutes later, Justin pushes through the door, and I blink ten times to be sure it's him. It's like I've been holding my breath for all this time, my back straight, my muscles tight, everything taut like an over-inflated balloon. Seeing him, alive, walking toward me, I deflate, curling in on myself. Tears storm the barricades. He's here; it's safe to feel all the things I was trying so hard not to feel but can't hold in any longer.

He's not dead; praise God.

But he could be.

I weep in the car in the dark on the way home. He cries, too. He says, "I'm sorry. I'll never be late again." But he will be. I'll plan his funeral while I wait on my running-late husband a dozen more times.

In these first months and even years after Bobby dies, I am convinced that everyone I love will die, probably in a car accident, probably today. Just months after Bobby dies I get a text plan on my phone for the first time. Texting allows me to keep constant vigil over my people. Texting also leads me into ten panic attacks a day when the person I'm texting can't text back because they're in a meeting or weighing fruit at the grocery store or giving their kids a bath. I type, "Are you okay??!!" Many. Times.

I'm not just certain the people I love will die suddenly, I'm also certain I will die suddenly, likely in a car accident. Or maybe of cancer. I find a lump in my breast and tell my doctor, and she feels it too and sends me to the ultrasound tech, and she says "hmm" and "huh" a lot as she takes grainy pictures, and I figure pictures must be bad. *Who takes pictures of nothing?* So for a while I think I'll die of breast cancer. But then they decide the lump is probably benign; I'm fine. I tell my mom and dad, who also thought I was probably dying. They've figured I'd die since my brother did. Mom sends more "Are you okay??!!" texts than I do. She calls me before road trips and begs me not to go. She gives me her credit card number so I'll stop and get a hotel. "It's a four-hour trip, Mom," I say. "You never know when you'll get tired," she says.

Maybe she's overreacting, but also she's not. Her daughter is dying. If not of cancer, then a car accident. And if not a car accident, something. Bobby's dying opens all of our eyes to the unavoidable fact that everyone, *everyone* is dying. Maybe in 50 years. Maybe today.

I'm reading this book about what it was like to live through the AIDS epidemic of the 1980s, and I find a story about two brothers. One has AIDS and the other doesn't. The one with AIDS says, "I'm going to die soon. I want you to know that." "I do," the brother without AIDS says. "You do know *what*?" says the brother with AIDS. "I know you're going to die." "Right," says the brother with AIDS, "But I'm surprised you don't know *you* are."

Grief, proximity to death, reminds any one of us how close death actually is. How powerful it is. How sneaky. When you lose a brother before he turns 21, when you stand next to a coffin and watch as it's pushed into a wall, knowing you just talked to the person inside last week... there's reorientation in a thing like that. It opens your eyes. Forces you to take a long look at what is. And very likely, pushed toe-to-toe with death, you'll discover you're afraid. Afraid of dying perhaps. Or maybe just afraid of being left behind.

I have this friend whose dad died suddenly of a heart attack when she was in high school. Her mom fell into heavy drinking, and this friend felt alone and vulnerable. She noticed she was becoming afraid of everything. She wrote to me, "The fear ranged from little things, like being unusually and irrationally afraid of the dark or spiders on a camping trip with friends, to big things, like that my boyfriend was bound to die unexpectedly." That second fear of hers was so strong she decided she needed to have sex with her boyfriend (even though she was certain it wasn't what God wanted for her) "because I wanted to experience all of him before he could die." She'd marry that boyfriend eventually, and the fear would continue so that she never wanted the two of them to be apart. Fear strangled her.

That's how it feels—like hands around your neck. For me, it felt like if I moved at all I'd be choked. Grief had unleashed a monster.

Most scary movies have the same plot:

First, the character is oblivious to the danger. She works as a lifeguard at the beach, laughing with friends after work, whiling away the hours in her chair uneventfully, drinking blueberry slurpees.

Second, the character becomes increasingly aware of something dark and mysterious. Someone is injured in the water but the wound doesn't look like a shark bite. *What could the creature be?* More people are hurt. People start to die.

Third, the character freaks out. She tries to quit her job as lifeguard. She calls her mom and cries uncontrollably. She has a panic attack while giving CPR to a victim.

Fourth, something moving happens that convinces the character to stick around and make a plan. Her little sister loses both legs and goes into shock. She decides to stay on as lifeguard and help the handsome guy with the boat and the other handsome guy with the hard-to-understand scientific theories.

Fifth, the character confronts the dark thing, mystery is dispelled, and the extent of the evil is observed. Miles away from land, they find the creature. It's a giant jellyfish with laser eyes. It lasers the handsome boat captain.

Sixth, the character makes a discovery and faces off against the evil. Having observed the handsome captain's death, she and the handsome scientist decide to gouge out the jellyfish's laser eyes. They grab random props from the boat deck and lure the jellyfish to the boat's edge.

Seventh, the character defeats the evil. Our lifeguard musters heroic courage, both impaling the jellyfish and saving the scientist from drowning. The beach town hosts a parade in her honor.

The end.

I am the lifeguard. Death is the jellyfish with laser eyes. I miss the blueberry slurpees.

~~~

Before you've met death face-to-face, you're oblivious to the danger. It's there, of course. Nothing changes in your stars when a person you love dies. It's just that suddenly you're made aware. You have to get a glimpse to be afraid.

Once you're made aware, it's like the lights flick on and you see death everywhere. You notice how many people on Facebook are grieving. You notice all the celebrities dying. You realize how dangerous everything is—driving, riding your bike, energy drinks. A friend almost dies when he falls into an electrified pool at a miniature golf course. Now I am afraid of miniature golf.

Before, I never thought about death. Post Bobby's dying, at least at first, I never think about much of anything else.

Eventually all the fear drives you somewhere. It makes you crazy or co-dependent or compulsive. You make your life small. You hesitate to make yourself vulnerable or take on risk. Or maybe you risk everything because you're bound to lose it anyway. You love less generously or less wisely. You wrap yourself in substances, thinking maybe if you can't feel it'll go away. Fear eats at you, consuming you, and soon enough you reach the point—the point when you decide to do something about it. Either that or you let it destroy you.

~~~

Fast forward a few years. Justin and I are headed to Dallas, just three or four hours up the road. At this point we have two toddler girls; they're staying with friends while we attend a work conference. Before the trip even begins I have decided our daughters will die while we're away. It isn't strange for me to feel this way, but what is strange is my inability to shake it. Checking into the hotel I'm restless; my stomach's turning over; my hands are clammy. Over dinner, I can't stop talking about death.

It's been six or seven years now since Bobby died. In that time I've miscarried three babies. I've lost both my grandfathers in the same month. I've had multiple cysts tested for breast cancer, including one biopsy performed in my sixth month of pregnancy. I say to Justin, in a poorly lit booth in a pub in a Dallas suburb, "I feel plagued by death." That is one part of what I'm feeling.

The other part is harder to put to words. I say, "I think maybe God wants me to write about death. Maybe that's my story." I weep as I contemplate this grim calling, imagining more people dying, quantifying how much more pain I will endure. At this moment I do not want to write about death. I want to forget about death. I want to walk away from death.

I'm the lifeguard in the scary story, calling home, deciding to quit my job and run away.

I realize the reason I am so affected, the reason I'm shaking and crying, is because this is the moment, the moment when I will have to decide which way to go—surrender or courage. And I prefer the ease of surrender.

I don't remember a lot about the conference I attend that weekend. I know I hear Brené Brown speak on vulnerability and courage. Her message is good, but it isn't until the end that she hooks me, when she reads the "Man in the Arena" speech from Teddy Roosevelt, a speech I now have hanging in my bedroom. She reads,

> The credit belongs to the man who is actually in the arena, whose face is marred by dust and sweat and blood; who strives valiantly; who errs, who comes short again and again, because there is no effort without error and shortcoming; but who does actually strive to do the deeds… who at the best knows in the end the triumph of high achievement, and who at the worst, if he fails, at least fails while daring greatly, so that his place shall never be with those cold and timid souls who neither know victory nor defeat.

I realize in this moment, I want to know victory.

Later, after this session, my husband and I will sit in our truck in the parking lot and cry. We will each share ways we've given up fighting, each commit to staying in the arena. I will realize it's time to start fighting death. I don't know exactly what that looks like yet, but I think it's more than trying not to be scared. I think an offense will be required.

Before we put the truck in drive, Justin tells me there's an Andrew Peterson concert in town, that he'd love for us to go. I don't know who Andrew Peterson is, so Justin pulls up a video on his phone and we watch this guy talking about tornadoes in Tennessee and how terrifying they are and how you never know when they're coming. And I think of death--powerful and scary. But Peterson is talking about God, the most powerful Force. Tornadoes remind him of God and how you never know when He'll come. He says, "I spend a lot of time wishing that God would unzip the air and step into our world and reveal himself himself to us." And then he sings about waiting for the second coming of this Force, this God who bends trees and lights up skies.

Fear has a lot to do with attention; I know this from being a parent. If my kids are scared of the dark, I tell them stories and they forget about the dark. If my kids are scared of the waves, I point to the seagulls overhead and their eyes lift above the water. If my kids are scared to be left at preschool, their teacher puts Play-Doh in their hands.

I realize now that I am looking at the wrong thing, that my attention is locked on Death. In this moment, I lift my eyes to something more powerful than Death: Life in Christ. I lift my eyes to the resurrection, the second coming, abundant, eternal Life. I imagine what it will be like, a forever with God, no pain, no disappointment, no conflict, no separation. I imagine what it could be like here, too, even now, a life defined by courage, joy, freedom, and hope. I decide to stop staring at the hourglass, sand falling, time passing, and start living now, outside of time, beyond it, straining my eyes to see the never-ending horizon. Maybe decide is the wrong word. Perhaps I am simply compelled. Compelled by God's power and love. Compelled by His proximity and promise. Compelled by the truth that Life will conquer Death, that it has already begun its advance.

I listen to Peterson singing about "the reckoning," the moment of curtain lifting, the moment the Kingdom breaks through, and I think of these words from the apostle Paul, words full of passion and confidence, words he wrote to people who overestimated Death. He wrote,

> Listen, I tell you a mystery: We will not all sleep, but we will all be changed—in a flash, in the twinkling of an eye, at the last trumpet. For the trumpet will sound, the dead will be raised imperishable, and we will be changed. For the perishable must clothe itself with the imperishable, and the mortal with immortality. When the perishable has been clothed with the imperishable, and the mortal with immortality, then the saying that is written will come

true: "Death has been swallowed up in victory." (I Corinthians 15:51–54)

Death has been swallowed up.
Death. Swallowed up.
In Victory.

I look at Death, and it's scary, but then I look at Life in Christ--immortality, imperishability, ultimate, eternal victory--and I wonder how I could ever have been so distracted by something so obviously outmatched.

We go to the concert that night. It's in an old white church building with stained glass. Every light is extinguished, but as the sun sets, pinks and purples and blues stream through, making almost-rainbows, crowning the audience in heavenly color. I don't know a single song. He doesn't sing the one we listened to in the car. But it doesn't matter. The songs are good background music for writing furiously in my notebook.

It is this night when this book you're holding is born. It doesn't look like this yet. It has a different title, a very defiant one. I write on the ivory page of my trusty moleskine: "Notes for a book on fighting death. Title: Damn Death." Below those words I make a plan to face my enemy.

I will decide later that perhaps some Christian men and women will feel awkward walking around with the word "damn" on their book, so I decide on the title "Swallowed Up." People will think I'm talking about grief, about the way it overtakes us, but I am in fact talking about Life in Christ and the victory-bringing power of resurrection.

It's true that grief made me afraid. But it's also true that grief made me brave. It dragged me into a confrontation that proved death's inferiority. When Bobby first died, I was afraid of dying, afraid of the people I loved dying. Death seemed larger than life. But now, having looked death in the eye, having fought back with life, life larger than death, I've realized death isn't so scary.

Death is a force with power, unquestionable power. Death corrupts. It weakens. It muzzles and chains. It despairs.

But what is death in this life when another life awaits, a life already beginning here and now, a life coming to fruition with the coming of Christ, a life that will never end?

Sickness here exhausts and pains and despairs, but even the longest of sicknesses here is but a second in scale when compared to infinity.

Loneliness here, loneliness born of loss, weighs heavy on our shoulders, but knowing that the loneliness won't last, that the time we spend without our people is infinitesimal in light of forever with our people—that lightens the load.

When I look through the filter of a holy, joy-soaked, peace-anchored forever, I see everything differently.

What if my parents die?

What if my children die?

What if my husband dies?

What if I die?

Well then, we die. And then we rise to live.

I don't know what Heaven is going to be like. I tend to agree with those who say it'll be an extension of Kingdom Life here, a completion of the good begun. I know there won't be tears. No broken relationships. No broken bodies. I know there won't be hate, only love. Sometimes I imagine Heaven as being a lot like Ireland, all green and alive, beside a wild and beautiful sea. Of course it won't be like Ireland entirely. The light will be better, fuller, brighter, never fading. I suspect we won't have rain.

There are days when I imagine what it will be like to see my brother. I imagine him and me swimming, swimming and never tiring, our glorified bodies tanned and glistening. We eat picnic lunches of grapes and honey and talk about our Holy Father and how much better He is than we'd ever hoped. I imagine Bobby will talk freely, finally unfettered, his self-awareness thrown off. I imagine us laughing and smiling straight smiles, both sides of our previously ever-crooked mouths upturned. I imagine singing with him and neither of us ever missing a note. I imagine singing and never even thinking of missed notes, our eyes locked on the Object of our love and song.

Lately I dream more about meeting God than anything else. I've become enraptured by His face. I imagine being held in His love, witnessing the full sunlight of His presence, exploring the fullness of His power.

These daydreams of forever empower me.

I won't let death stand in the way of me living the abundant life Christ promised. I'm not afraid to die. Not at all. I'm not afraid of my kids dying. Or my husband. Death has nothing to ransom.

And that makes me dangerous.

When you reach the fork in the road, the choice between courage and surrender, your decision will be made in direct correlation to the focus of your gaze. *Look at God. Look at life. Look at life forever. And death won't loom so large.*

PART 3

Surf

noun:

the swell of the sea that breaks upon a shore

JANUARY 30, 2004

It's funny how no matter what I start to write everything comes back to Bobby.

CHAPTER 10

FALLING, IN LOVE

"Most of all, love each other as if your life depended on it. Love makes up for practically anything."

I Peter 4:8, *The Message*

Last summer I took the first chapter of this book to a writing workshop in Minnesota. I gathered around a table with eleven other writers, all strangers, and together we inspected one another's words. We looked closely, poked and prodded. It was kind of them to read my sad sentences. After we'd considered my chapter, I had a few people come up to me and ask questions. Some wanted to know more about my brother, but everyone, every single person, wanted to know more about my marriage. "You were so young," my new friend Bromleigh said, her face wide with amazement. "You have to write more about that," she continued—more about what it was like to be married, grieving, and too young to rent a car. Her face said, "How was that not a disaster?"

The official statistics vary, but according to the Center for Disease Control and Prevention, 48 percent of those who marry before 18 are likely to divorce within 10 years—that's compared with 24 percent of those who marry after age 25. I'd heard these stats in high school, back when I was 18 and had been dating my now-husband for four years. We waited until I turned 19 to get married. Seemed like the wise thing to do.

I'm thinking of that tonight, lying next to my husband in the bed, when I ask him, "Why are we still married?"

It's a reasonable question to ask about a pair like us, married too early, total opposites, crushed by grief so early in our relationship. The odds say we shouldn't be together. Sometimes we say we shouldn't be together—at least, on paper.

It's been two years since Bobby died, two years and change, when I almost die in a car accident. I say "almost die" because I could have died, but instead I climb out of my totaled car basically unscathed. I tried to cross a busy street, thought I had time, and missed an oncoming truck. The truck driver didn't have time to even hit his brakes. He smashed into my rear passenger side at full speed and spun me around until I crashed into a car waiting to cross on the other side. Hitting that car propelled me into a ditch. I missed a utility pole by inches.

I don't remember much from the accident, but I do remember the woman I hit helping me out of my car. I remember her saying, "I saw the whole thing; it was like God picked up your car and put it down in just the right spot." She said, "You should have hit that pole," and "I don't understand why your car didn't roll over." She said, "It's a miracle you're alive."

The weekend of the accident, Justin and I tag along with friends on a trip to Boone, North Carolina, to snowboard. Raised in Florida, neither Justin nor I have snowboarded before. We wakeboard though. We've surfed. Our friends say it'll be easy.

I almost back out of the trip. I tell Justin I can't do it. I'm bruised. My whole body feels sore. But more than that, I'm feeling breakable. I'm feeling like I might crack. I decide to go because Justin wants to go and because I don't want to be left alone.

We wait in long lines to get our gear. Our friends explain how to put it on and then offer a quick orientation to snowboarding. Seems easy enough. We ride a lift to the baby hill and set out. Justin is good immediately. I am too careful, too quick to slow down, too nervous. I can't keep my balance. I fall a lot.

Justin sticks with me for a while, but I can tell he's eager to stretch his legs on harder runs. Normally this wouldn't bother me. I don't mind being alone. I like watching him excel at things. But today feels different. Today I can't stop crying. Working my way down this slope has me weeping. I'm cold. I'm hurting. I'm embarrassed at how bad at this I am. I'm mad at our friends for trying to help me. I'm a mess.

On my second attempt I find myself paralyzed. I sit down in the snow and cry. I refuse to budge. This is not characteristic of me. I don't know why I'm so shaken and afraid. Justin sits down beside me, and I say through sobs, "I just feel so fragile." He convinces me to make my way down the slope. He says, "You can scoot the whole way down if you need to." He's kind and helpful. He says at the bottom, "Why don't you go get a hot chocolate in the lodge?"

Hot chocolate sounds good, but what I want is security. I want a person to sit with me and make me feel safe. I want to talk through what I'm feeling and try to figure it out. I really want to go home.

Justin, though—he really wants to snowboard. He asks if I mind if he goes with our friends. I say, "Go ahead." I say "go ahead," but I don't want him to go. I expect that he should gather this on his own. I want him to want to stay with me. But he doesn't want to stay with me. He wants to learn how to snowboard.

And so he leaves me alone.

After I drink my hot chocolate and jot some things down in a notebook, trying to sort my feelings, I go looking for Justin, but can't find him. I watch every man, woman, and child coming down the slopes. I strain my eyes looking for his putty-colored coat. I look for an hour and can't find him. Eventually I find one of our friends, and she helps me find him. He's happy and proud and oblivious. He tells me to wait at the bottom and watch his run.

This is the story Justin remembers when I ask him about grief and our marriage. I say, "Can you think of a time when we didn't understand one another? A time when we failed each other in grief?" He's still for a long time. Then he says, "Remember that time we went snowboarding right after your accident?"

Facing grief early in our marriage forced us into a quick realization of our incompatibility. We saw differences in the ways we'd been wired and raised, differences in the ways we handled stress, differences in our priorities, differences in the ways we wanted to be loved. I think we could have gone years, maybe decades, without seeing what we saw in the aftermath of loss.

When my grief led to depression, we discovered that Justin didn't know how to handle it. He liked fixing things, making things better and happier. He wanted to fix me, and I didn't want to be fixed. His only other way of handling something heavy like this was to ignore it, but with depression seeping into everything, how could he?

For Justin, grief stirred up an appetite for people and parties. He needed connection, fun, pleasure, and I couldn't understand that need at all. He'd want to go out for dinner with friends, want to eat something interesting and delicious. I just wanted to order pizza and stay home. He'd start kissing me in bed after a hard conversation, and I'd wonder, "How can you want sex at a time like this?" He couldn't understand why I'd reject him, him feeling so vulnerable and sad, so eager to connect with another human.

In grief, I reached for order and work and routine, ways of controlling my out-of-control life. I set bedtimes and wake-times for both of us. I made arbitrary diet decisions. I overloaded our lives with obligations. Justin bristled at my rules and expectations. He stayed up past my bedtimes and slept in past my wake-times. He despised being told what to do.

In the wake of loss, I decided I wanted a baby. Justin wondered how I could think of adding one more hard thing to our life. Justin wanted to dream about a new job and new city, imagine what we might do next, but I felt oppressed and overwhelmed by his plans.

We both wished someone would do the dishes.

Every day we were reminded that this person we'd married was confounding and disappointing. If those realizations had come at another time, we'd have handled them differently, perhaps we'd have seen them as bigger, more consequential. But because they came in the middle of a storm, both of us holding onto the other, so afraid to let go, we didn't let go. We still haven't.

~~~

When I ask Justin, "Why are we still married?" he puts his arm behind his head, looks up at the ceiling and thinks. Silently. For many long seconds. I hate it when he thinks alone in his head instead of out loud in real-time, but I'm learning to let the man think how he wants to think. So he thinks, and then he says, lifting his words from the quiet, "We were never enemies."

I don't understand what he means immediately, so he explains. He says in grief, you're so angry, ready to blame anyone close for your pain. He said we were definitely in pain, definitely angry and sad, but we never blamed each other; we never saw the other person as an opponent or obstacle. "We've always been partners," he says.

He reminds me of something I found in an old journal. I'm writing about attending a family reunion in 2004, just the second reunion since Bobby died. Reflecting on the first day back home, a heavy day full of grief, I write, "Last night Justin and I had a pity party. We cried together about Bobby—we both missed him so much at the reunion." *We cried together.* A few sentences later: "It was good to yell and not to be yelling at each other."

I guess the reason I'm still married, despite the grief and our immaturity and differences, is this: When things got hard, death didn't turn us against each other. In the face of loss, we held hands and braved it together.

~~~

Together is harder for people who're different. Sameness is attractive because it's easy. But even as difference is hard, it's also undeniably better. Our differences, when we accept them and understand them, make our marriage full and round. We're better partners because we're different.

Justin and I recently ran across the enneagram—essentially, a personality-typing system that assigns people numbers. You've probably heard all about it. We picked up a book a few months ago and figured out our types. If you know enneagram, I'm either a Four or a One. That means I'm a moody, self-loathing idealist who works too hard, always meets deadlines, and thinks no one understands her. Justin's a Seven. Sevens are irrepressibly fun, curious, and ambitious. They're good at everything except time management. They live in the future and struggle to stay.

After we'd figured out our types, I Googled "relationship between Four and Seven." I found this: "Enneagram Fours and Sevens tend to be intrigued by each other since they are generally a case of opposites attracting." I laughed but wasn't surprised. As I kept reading, I saw a lot of phrases like "Sevens help Fours overcome..." and "Fours help Sevens stay..." The short description ended with the words, "Being opposites, Fours and Sevens can balance each other."

I thought, That's exactly it. When my brother and Justin's best friend hit a tree and died, when that wave crashed down on both our heads, we held each other tightly, our four feet more sturdy than any two on their own. We balanced each other.

Justin helped me embrace the delights of friendship and adventure. He reminded me that sadness and joy can coexist. He helped me imagine a better tomorrow. He pulled me out of the bed when I really did need to get up.

I helped Justin learn how to deal with his feelings. I taught him how to stay in a moment, how to embrace hard things and grow. I slowed him down when he needed to dial it back. I encouraged discipline.

We were, we are, more together than we are alone.

The writer of Ecclesiastes says, "Two are better than one… if either of them falls down, one can help the other up. But pity anyone who falls and has no one to help them up." (4:9–10) How many times have I fallen? How many times have I let death get the best of me, push me down, hold me there? And how many times has my husband reached down to help me up?

These days, whenever Justin lets me down, whenever I do something stupid and disappoint his reasonable expectations, we have a lot grace. Surviving loss taught us that it's not perfection you want in a marriage. It's partnership.

My husband, God bless him, doesn't like dogs. At all. He doesn't like the mess, doesn't like the work, doesn't like being tied down by feeding schedules and finding a friend to watch the dog when you're out of town. I do like dogs. I like dogs because I like to be wanted and admired. I like dogs because they need you, because they crawl into your lap and lick the tears off your cheeks.

One night in February, a little over a year after Bobby died, Justin told me about a litter of chocolate lab puppies just across the state line in Tennessee. He'd seen an ad in the paper. He drove me 45 minutes north so I could hold one. We pulled up to the house, an old house on a big green field. The sky was cloudy. The air cold. I sat on the grass and let puppies crawl all over me—a perfect moment. I found the one I wanted. Justin hadn't exactly meant to buy a puppy that night. I think he'd meant for me to look, to maybe pick one for later. But seeing me so happy, he ran to the closest Walmart, bought a carrier and dog food and a collar, and came back to get my dog.

The puppy rode in my lap for the 45-minute trek home. He barked the whole way and peed on my jeans. That night, a Saturday night, the night before Justin would have to preach, my new dog barked from 9 p.m. to 6 a.m.

For the next two years, Abe (full name Abraham) would do everything in his power to make Justin's life difficult. He ran away from home periodically. He ate all our grill paraphernalia. He pooped everywhere. He snuck into our bed and left dog hairs on our pretty white comforter.

One night, sitting on the couch with my legs draped over Justin's, I said, "You know, I don't have Abe's exact birthdate, but I was figuring it out today, and there's a really good chance Abe was born on December 13th. Isn't that crazy?"

Justin smiled, laughed a little. I leaned in and put my head on his shoulder. We sat there, me thinking of the gift of this dog, of my husband's sacrifice to love me, him thinking of the gift of his happier wife via this dog he'd learned to endure.

CHAPTER 11

GOOD THINGS

"The pupil dilates in darkness and in the end finds light, just as the soul dilates in misfortune and in the end finds God."

Victor Hugo, *Les Misérables*

Within the first week of my brother dying, I've already imagined how sad it will be to give birth to my kids without Bobby in the waiting room. I'm not pregnant. I'm not planning on having kids anytime soon. But already I've jumped ahead five years to imagine how sad it will be. I think that's a normal thing to do when you're grieving, to look ahead and saddle the future with sadness. In the moment, I think it's inevitable. *Nothing will ever be happy again, even the happiest thing I can imagine. All of life is ruined.*

Three years later I will miscarry two babies, more sadness stealing any chance at one-day happiness.

I find out I'm pregnant with London while living in Brooklyn. My husband and I are there to plant a church. It's been a rough nine months, what with the miscarriages, the death of our second dog, Isaac, the death of Justin's grandmother, the turmoil at our home church in Alabama, and, of course, the loneliness of living in a new, very big place. We don't know if the pregnancy will stick, but we tell people about it anyway. Because we hope it will. Because we want prayers. And because we're happy.

We walk down the street to a baby boutique and buy a onesie with the words "Made in Brooklyn" across the tiny chest. We go to a Tyrone Wells concert in some cramped club on the Lower East Side, and I wonder if she can hear (she can't; it's much too early). I shop for easy-to-fold strollers for getting up and down subway stairs.

About seven weeks into our pregnancy, morning sickness in full swing, we find out the family who's been funding our church work in New York can't support us anymore. It's 2007, he's a financial planner, and the economy is tanking. Suddenly we're jobless in the second-most expensive city in the country. Also, our lease is up in two weeks.

You can't make this stuff up.

We eventually have to leave Brooklyn and move to the small town in Tennessee where we attended college. It's a breathtaking transition. We buy a big white house with a wide brick porch, and I lie, five months pregnant, in the back bedroom on an air mattress waiting for our things, because the moving company sent them to the wrong state.

The whole time, London is growing inside me, and though I'm sick almost every day (I lose fifteen pounds in the first trimester), and though I'm sad most days, too (this is not the life I would have chosen), I also find myself growing in joy, lit from the inside like a lantern.

I hold London's little baby clothes, all yellow and green and white because we don't know if she's a she or a he. I pack my hospital bag with Blow Pops and a portable speaker and a cozy robe. I buy her books. I read to her from the book of John every night. I dream of her floating peacefully in an amniotic fluid aquarium, me pressed up against the glass, straining to get a better look.

Some nights, my belly round like a rising sun, I sneak into her nursery to sit in the chair where I'll soon hold her in my arms. I sit in the quiet in that beautiful room—white fur rug, chocolate-brown walls decorated with black-and-white portraits of our parents, a perfect crib I picked out with my grandfather, a bookcase eight feet squared packed with my favorite stories. I sit in the perfect quiet and I open myself up to joy.

A week before London is due, the tub overflows and floods the bathroom. I text Justin, who calls the plumber. I gather all the towels from the house and sop up the mess. I finish, get up off my knees, and walk to the hallway, and my water breaks. I laugh at the puddle on the floor. I have not one dry towel in the whole house.

Justin comes home from work to take me to the hospital. I have time to wash and dry my hair, to put on makeup, to check the bag once or twice. We may or may not grab a chai tea latte on the way. When we get to the hospital, labor is long (nineteen hours), frustrating (I'm told I can't deliver naturally, induction required, my midwife isn't available), and painful (those induction drugs are no joke), but eventually I'm given an epidural and I take a much-needed nap. I wake to a room streaming with morning light and a kind doctor telling me it's almost time to push.

I freshen my lipstick and suck on a Blow Pop while the nurses get things ready. Justin hooks up the speaker to his iPod and holds my hand.

London is born in three pushes to Jack Johnson singing, "We got everything we need right here. And everything we need is enough."

The doctor says, "It's a girl," and lays all nine pounds of London Jane Gerhardt on my chest. Justin, tears glistening on his cheeks, leans down to kiss me and kiss her and kiss me.

Just so easy when the whole world fits inside of your arms.

I am happier than I have ever, ever been.

I'm not only happy when London is born. I do miss Bobby. I miss him especially when my friend Matt is the first person to the hospital, the first person besides me and Justin to hold her. Matt and I are friends because Bobby died, because his dad died and he came to me looking for hope and a friend. Matt, just three years younger than Bobby, grins from ear to ear, holding our little girl, so afraid of breaking her, so delighted by her tiny hands and the dimple in her chin.

Matt makes me miss my brother. And Matt, my brother in grief and new brother in Christ, fills the room with light.

Happy. Sad. Happy.

In the years since Bobby died, Justin and I have built a whole life, so much of it different than the life we lived with Bobby. We've moved across the country three times. We've said goodbye to friends. We've made new friends. We have two amazing kids. Our bodies are more tired than they once were, but we've grown in faith and wisdom and kindness. We've learned lots of new skills. Our jobs are different. Our hobbies are different. We eat sushi now. And Indian food. And salads at least once a week. We send GIFs on our iPhones (Bobby would have loved

GIFs—and iPhones).

Sometimes I'm tempted to look at that life and see all the places where Bobby should have been, all the things he missed, all the times I missed him. Ann Voskamp writes in her book *One Thousand Gifts*, "One life-loss can infect the whole of a life. Like a rash that wears through our days, our sight becomes peppered with black voids. Now everywhere we look, we only see all that isn't: holes, lack, deficiency."

But that's no way to live a life, letting loss blind us to joy.

Maybe you feel like you're supposed to be sad all the time. Maybe you feel like your sadness is a tribute to the person you loved, like the sadder you are, the more you must have loved. I get that. I felt that. I'm not telling you to buck up and get cheery. This sadness you feel may last your whole life (though I'm certain you'll feel it less oppressively one day).

What you need to hear is this: Life can be both happy and sad. You can suffer and celebrate. You can cry and laugh. You can love the him who died and love a new him, too. You can wish she was here and still enjoy here.

If I've learned anything in my brother's death, this is it. Life will be devastatingly sad sometimes. And other times life will feel like champagne in your veins. Be sad. And be happy. What a mistake it would be to only feel one.

The apostle Paul says to the Philippians, "Rejoice in the Lord always. I will say it again: Rejoice!" (4:4) He tells them this in the middle of their (and his) intense suffering. He tells them to rejoice while they suffer, knowing that suffering without joy is too hard, too heavy. He says, a couple verses later, "Brothers and sisters, whatever is true, whatever is noble, whatever is right, whatever is pure, whatever is lovely, whatever is admirable—if anything is excellent or praiseworthy—think about such things." (4:8) Paul says, *Don't just look at what's hard and sad and wrong and missing. Lift your eyes, and find what's light and happy and good and here.*

Surviving this grief, then, means opening myself up to joy. It means deciding that life can be good, that in so many ways it already is. Paul's recipe for joy in suffering is an exercise in looking not for the holes and voids but rather for the fullness, the blessings, the excess. It's practicing the discipline of remembering, remembering good times and God's presence. It's actively pursuing thanksgiving for today's gifts, noticing the food in your fridge and the friends on your block and the phone beside your bed, connecting you to people you love, people who love you. It's acknowledging the goodness all around you, owning the gift of your life.

Though I am sad, I am giving myself permission to be happy—to welcome new adventures, to embrace beautiful moments, to pursue connection, to learn new things. When I do this in the face of loss, I build a life that though less is also more—more full, more holy. Yes, there are holes and longings and empty chairs around my table. But there are also great, luxurious, undeserved glories, blessings that come when I choose to stay alive and keep living.

I pray with Gerard Manley Hopkins, "Glory be to God for dappled things"—for this dappled life, all joys and shadows, loss and gain, both.

I'm sleeping, and Bobby wakes me up. He's dead, so I know he's not actually waking me up. I wonder for a second, but then—of course… A dream. Bobby tells me he has something for me, that he left me something and I have to find it. I tell him, *I did.* I found the sweatshirt. It was in a plastic bag from our college bookstore, the sweatshirt I'd told him I wanted the last time I saw him, at Thanksgiving, when our friend Michael was wearing one. I said I wanted a large, something comfy and cozy. He told me girls look pregnant and homeless in size large sweatshirts. He said my clothes should fit. Among Bobby's things I'd found the bag and the size-small sweatshirt. A gift.

He tells me there's more. He's excited and in a rush. In the dream I search my whole house. I open drawers and pull everything out of my closet. I remember a dresser with seemingly endless compartments. I wake up having found nothing, but I'm not disappointed. I've seen Bobby. And he left me something.

The next time I go to Florida, I tell my mom and dad I want to go the site of the wreck. I haven't been yet. I don't tell them Bobby left me something in case it's not there, in case they think I'm crazy. But that's the reason I want to go. When we get there, we walk down off the highway and into the tree line, toward the tree marked by the impact. You can still find shards of glass, pieces of car debris, but all of Bobby's belongings are gone—friends have been to this site every day, of course there's nothing left. Still, I search, eyes darting across the ground, hungry for this thing I'm promised.

Then I see something: a turtle shell. I reach down to pick it up and, fingers touching plastic, I realize this is it. It's a toy, a plastic and latex turtle with the head cut off. Bobby cut off the head intentionally. He kept the turtle in his car so that when he pulled up to a light he could stick his finger into the latex body, lift the turtle, and make it look like he'd been bitten. Once he had the attention of a neighboring driver, Bobby would shake his hand wildly as if the turtle had bitten him and wouldn't let go.

I tenderly tuck the plastic turtle, a treasure, into my jacket pocket. I never was much fun growing up. I suspect this is Bobby's way of telling me to lighten up.

In six years, I'll attach that plastic turtle to my finger and surprise my two-year-old. She will be delighted, her giggles like bubbles filling the room. She'll put it on her own finger and giggle some more. I'll tell her the turtle was her Uncle's Bobby's turtle. I'll tell her it was his joke. She'll run to the library and come back hugging his framed picture.

CHAPTER 12

WAVES

"For whatever we lose (like a you or a me), it's always our self we find in the sea."

e. e. cummings, "maggie and milly and molly and may"

I'm holding my daughter London's hand, our faces salty and browned on this our fourth day at Padre Island National Seashore. We call this place Texas Beach. It's easier for little girls to say. London is three, Eve two. We can't afford a vacation, but our friends have a timeshare here. It's not as lovely as the Florida Gulf Coast beaches we grew up on, but it's a beach, and the beach resets me. It sounds and tastes and smells like home.

I've been grieving Bobby for almost ten years now. The grief is more muted. Less oppressive. But life hasn't stopped handing me things to grieve. My grandfather's dying. I grew up in his house; he's more second-father than grandfather. My last trip to see him, he couldn't get out of bed. He's having strokes now. The doctor says eventually he'll die from one. I held his hand and read him one of my recent blog posts. We sang and prayed and cried. I don't want to say goodbye, and I don't want to see him in so much pain.

I'm grieving some other things, too, losses of one kind or another. On this very trip our one family car has broken down. We have no money to fix it and have to leave it in San Antonio. A family at our church hears the news and pays for a rental car. Another friend offers to pay for the repair. Light in the dark.

I pick up London and carry her into the water. The waves are high for the Gulf, high and choppy. We're struck again and again by punches of crashing sea. London, angry, tells the waves to "stop it." I am in a melancholy mood and can't help turning these waves into metaphor. I decide these waves are losses, and I am being attacked by them, assailed. I want to give up on trying. I want to get out of this oppressive water beating me down.

But then I remember being a little girl in Florida, swimming with my parents, water glistening on their smiling faces, my mom floating on her back, my dad holding me in his strong, relaxed arms. I remember the way we'd embrace the waves, the familiar rhythm of up and down, up and down. Then I remember learning to surf, how you could wear yourself out trying to fight the waves or you could just dive into them, pushing under the water to avoid being pulled backward. Finally I remember the number one rule of ocean-swimming: Don't fight nature.

I tell my daughter to hold tight, lift my feet from the ground, and let the wave carry us. I look over at London as we're lifted by the swell, and her face turns from grimace to giggle: "*Weeeee...*"

We spend an hour in the water, up and down, up and down, up and down.

Later that night, I'll think of this moment and wonder if there's some wisdom in it for me. I wonder if there's a way to submit to my suffering without letting it win, a way to let it lift me.

I make two lists in my journal: one of ways I've been struck down and one of ways I've been lifted. Both lists are long. In the moment, I am only thankful for the lifting list. Looking back at the lists today, I can see things to be thankful for on the crashing side, ways God's used those pains to shape me and grow me, ways God's used what seemed hard to protect me from something harder, ways God's used those losses to make space for future gains.

I realize that as scary and exhausting as the waves may be, God is with me in the water and God is working in the waves.

Perhaps the way to embrace a wave is to stop fighting so hard to stand on your own two feet, stop trying to make the waves go away, and instead lift your feet off the ocean floor, trusting that even waves can be lifting.

After that day at the beach, we cooked Gulf-caught shrimp on the small gas stove in our loaner-condo. We sat around a small glass table, the girls barely contained in their wicker seats. We asked London to pray. She prayed, "Thank you, God, for waves."

I'm looking at a painting by the famous Russian marine painter Ivan Aivazovsky. Most art historians say Aivazovsky was better at painting the ocean than anyone who ever lived. This painting is arguably his best. It's called "The Ninth Wave," a reference to the legend that the "ninth wave," the last wave, was the most powerful and destructive. In it, a band of shipwrecked sailors cling to their ship's mast as massive waves surround and threaten them. The painting finds its hope in a rising sun. The night is over. Perhaps they'll live.

It's been noted that the ship's mast, the wood to which these sailors hold, seems intentionally painted to resemble a cross, and that the rising sun represents God's presence and provision in storms.

While Aivazovsky clearly excels in painting water and waves, it's not the waves that make this painting special. It's the sun and the way light illuminates the cresting water. Opaque and flat in the dark, the waves come to life in the morning. Translucent, unveiled, they seem less dangerous.

As I look for the ninth wave in this painting, the wave that's most powerful, the wave that comes last, I wonder if perhaps Aivazovsky isn't referring to a literal wave at all. Though the waves are high, they only compose one-third of the visual landscape. Two-thirds are devoted to sky and sun. The rising sun is the first place your eye lands, and clearly the heart of the painting. Light touches every inch of canvas.

I think maybe the ninth wave is the sun, God, all-powerful, lifting those men even in the storm, lifting them to life, swallowing up death with light.

CHAPTER 13

MILE MARKER 15

"And will I tell you that these three lived happily ever after? I will not, for no one ever does. But there was happiness. And they did live."

Stephen King, *The Dark Tower*

I'm in a plane headed to Florida via Georgia to be with my parents on the occasion of the 15th anniversary of my brother's death. I'm wearing my "I will not be shaken" t-shirt and reading about the resurrection. I didn't plan it that way. It's where I am in my daily reading of John. Yesterday, crucifixion. Today, an empty tomb.

My goal for this trip is what? To remember? To mark the moment? To say something happened and it mattered? Partly it's to be with my parents, to stand on the same ground, to hold hands if it shakes.

My flight to Florida on the day Bobby died took all day, almost 20 hours in a plane or an airport. The clouds were dark, heavy with rain, lit by thunder. I flew through the same storm my brother had driven through, the same storm that had made the roads wet and slippery, the storm that had made his drive longer, outlasting his energy and focus. I arrived past midnight. As I will tonight.

Today the skies are clear, no clouds. As I fly over Alabama, I can see the quilted fields, rooftops, rivers, cows if I squint. The sun shines so bright the view is overexposed.

This is different, this trip. For one, I'm not crying. *I still might.* But these days tears are usually friends, reminders, gifts of joy, markers of being alive and able to feel. They haven't always been that way. Once, they held me hostage.

My plans upon arrival are to spend time with my mom and dad, to go to Bobby's grave, to drive out to the wreck site. I've made a list of questions to ask my parents. I hope to read them the first few chapters of this book. Maybe I'm going to Florida to see if what I've written feels true there, closer to the epicenter.

The Bible in my lap is open. I put away my pen-scratched plans and pick up the reading. Mary has gone to the tomb "while it is still dark," and I am thinking of how resurrection always comes at just that time, when maybe it seems like morning has run away and won't return. I remember the "still dark," and I give thanks for a rising sun.

I notice that God has moved the stone. Or His angels. I'm glad Mary didn't have to muster the strength herself.

I move on to Peter and John, running, arriving, Peter rushing inside, staring at the burial strips. John says, "He saw and believed."

I wonder, "What are the chances I'll find my brother's tomb empty tomorrow?" Not great.

But because this tomb is empty, this tomb on this page, I'm not in a hurry. Empty is coming…

I bought this flight months ago from Frontier Airlines for 90% off. I can't say it's wise to buy 90%-off airline tickets. A few days before I leave, I realize the flight I booked is impossible. I'll get into Orlando at midnight and then have to drive to Pinellas County, pull in close to 2 a.m., spend the day doing hard, emotional things, and then drive back at 3 in the morning. I tell my husband, and he says, "You need to add a day to that itinerary so you're not too tired to drive." Then he pauses. "Wouldn't it be whack if you died on your trip to remember your brother dying?"

This is where we are now. We use the word "whack" to describe ironic dying.

I add a day, but the hours stay the same. I fly from Austin to Atlanta early and then wait in Atlanta for five hours, writing. About ten minutes before my plane begins to board, I decide to look up my rental car reservation. *Weird.* I don't have an email about a rental car. Then I remember getting distracted while I was making the reservation; so I make a new one. And as I hit the reserve button, I remember: I don't have my driver's license. I lost it a week before and am flying with my passport.

I call my parents. I say, "I can't rent a car without my license." My mom calls the rental car place, tries to convince them to let me use my license number. They tell her it's a decision someone will have to make at the airport location, and she calls me back and says, "Good luck." She and dad can't come get me. It's too late. I cross my fingers and board my plane.

When I get to Orlando, I can't rent a car. I am really nice to the car rental man, but he tells me this is airport policy. He can't override it. I ask what I should do. He has no tips.

I Google. There's no train to Pinellas County. The Greyhound bus leaves at 5 in the morning. I think maybe I'll sleep in the airport, take a taxi to the bus station early, and take the bus to my parents. But then I realize I'm outside security, and the airport people will kick me out if I try to loiter—I'll have to get a hotel. Finally, I stumble on Uber.

I've never Uber-ed before, but I download the app, figure out the estimated price (less than a hotel room), and text my husband, who is in a very important meeting and can't talk. I tell him to pray for my safety and to call me when he gets out. I call my mom and tell her my Uber driver's name and license plate number. And then I get in a stranger's car, in a city where I know no one, at 11:24 p.m. I ride in the dark with Pedro for almost two hours.

And for two hours, I am gloriously and supernaturally at peace, just as I've been all day. I should be stressed. Or afraid. Or sad. Or overwhelmed. Things didn't go right. This wasn't how it was supposed to be. I'm spending $100 right after I added a day to the flight and busted the budget. I won't have a car while I'm here. Who knows how I'll get back to Orlando to fly out? Add to all of that the emotional load of hours of writing about my dead brother.

I should be bothered.

But I just feel peace. A peace that doesn't make sense. Ever since my brother died, God's been growing this peace in me, a peace I never had before. The apostle Paul says, "the peace of God, which transcends all understanding, will guard your hearts and your minds in Christ Jesus." (Philippians 4:7) It's true. I feel guarded, safe.

I arrive past 1 a.m. at my mom and dad's. I thank Pedro for not being a serial killer. I don't say that explicitly, but I think he gets my drift.

I knock on the front door and wake my mom, who's sleeping by the door. Her daughter's driving across the state late at night with a stranger, and she's sleeping. She is Jesus in the boat in the storm.

We've both come so far.

I spend my first day in Florida, the day before the death anniversary, with my mom at work. Mom directs a program that empowers autistic young adults by providing training in basic social and workplace skills. She teaches them how to cook. She gets them jobs. Today we are going Christmas caroling.

When we arrive at the school, her students are already waiting. She walks in the door and they greet her with riotous enthusiasm. They see me and immediately know who I am (though I've never been to this class before). "Jennifer!!" they yell, like we're old friends reunited. One student wants a hug. He's wearing a Lion King t-shirt and a Santa hat and talks too loudly. Another wants a picture. She's wearing antlers and a Rudolph nose and won't quite make eye contact.

I watch them practice for the caroling. Mom tells them to sing out, to look up, to smile. Empirically, they are terrible singers. Some rush ahead. Some fall behind. Hardly any are singing the same notes. Many of the words are hard to understand. But their excitement charges the songs with electric life and joy. They sing "Joy To The World," and I cry.

Later today, I'll watch them sing at retirement homes and nursing facilities, and some of the elderly audience members won't quite know what to do with them, but others will wear smiles too big for their faces. A nurse hugs every one of the students as they leave. An elderly woman walks up on the stage and sings the entire set with the group.

It isn't perfect, this performance. It's not even "good." But it's beautiful.

When Bobby died, mom was a sixth-grade reading teacher. After Bobby died, she finished a master's degree and worked as an assistant principal, then a principal. She's known for turning around struggling schools. Later, she'd devote herself to kids on the margins, orphans and autistic young adults.

I don't know that Mom would have thrown herself into her career so fully if Bobby hadn't died. Maybe. I do know that since he's died, she's blossomed.

The same's true for my dad. When Bobby died, Dad was still working for Coca-Cola delivering Cokes. It was the same job he'd worked since he was nineteen. Not too long after Bobby's wreck, Dad retired and took a job as a dorm parent at the college Bobby and I attended. He cooked for those boys, he helped fix their cars, he played ping pong with them, and he and prayed with them and gave advice-packed speeches (much like the ones he gave Bobby). I think Dad's losing his son enabled him to be a kind of father to those young men, hundreds of them. Most of them are married now. They have kids. They send my parents Christmas cards and call to catch up. They still call him Papa Bill.

Bobby's dying was the worst thing that ever happened to our family. There's no making it something good. Jerry Sittser says in his book about the tragic loss of his wife and child, "The good that may come out of loss does not erase its badness or excuse the wrong done." That's true. And simultaneously it is true that God works in the wreckage to redeem our pain.

There's a cleverness to God's methods, His refusal to let death have the final say. Even when death wins a skirmish,

God's shaping the fallout, collecting the broken pieces and using them for holy purposes.

If Bobby hadn't died, I don't know that I would have been such a good friend to Margaret, an elderly woman from my Alabama church, dying of cancer. I sat with her, painted her fingernails, listened to her tell stories from her dreams. I wouldn't have been equipped to sit with Amy's little girls while their mom planned their dad's unexpected funeral.

Bobby's dying made me strong enough to sit with death.

If Bobby hadn't died, I wouldn't have talked about my grief in my World Lit. class during a Tolstoy lecture, and my student Matt wouldn't have asked me to tell him more after class. His dad had recently died, and our common grief drew us together. Over time, Matt started going to church with me and studying with Justin, and now he is my brother. My girls were flower girls in his wedding.

If Bobby hadn't died, I would not have written this book.

I'm not of the mind that God took Bobby in order to accomplish these things in and through my family. If He did, I accept that. I accept whatever God does; He's God. But I suspect, knowing what I do of God's nature, that it's far more likely these victories were accomplished in response to Bobby's death, a sort of counterattack from the forces of Life against the forces of Death, a counterattack rising from the wreckage of Death's ultimately empty victory.

After work, Mom and Dad host a party to celebrate my aunt and uncle's 40th wedding anniversary. All three of my mom's brothers come, their wives, two of my cousins. We eat chicken and dumplings and chocolate cake. We play The Newlywed

Game. We tell stories. Everyone is happy, engaged. I think of how delighted my grandparents would be to see this, their children together, every one of them living in the same city, all of them laughing. I am tempted in this moment to be jealous of this beautiful, precious thing, jealous of siblinghood, jealous of growing up and growing old with people who know your stories. But tonight, the feeling is only a temptation because, more than anything, I feel like I belong, like these are my people, like these stories are ours.

As the night wears on, the stories grow more serious. We talk about marriage and how hard it is to make love last. My cousin encourages everyone to pray more for their husbands and wives. She regrets not praying enough for her ex-husband. My mom cries, remembering how scared she was after Bobby died that her marriage would be in danger. As a teenage bride, the odds were already stacked against her. Now, losing a child, she worried, would be too much. She says God led them through like He led Israel through the wilderness.

My Uncle Tim talks about discovering his melanoma and being given a prognosis of less than a year to live. He leans back on the oversized couch looking fit and handsome, his blue eyes bright, no detectable cancer in his body. He says, "Something so drastic happens and it reminds you to look at every day and enjoy it." I think he will talk about being healed and how thankful he is, but instead he says he's so glad to be reminded he's dying. Still dying. Always headed toward dying. He says he's a better person living a better life because he knows we're all dying.

We decide to end this holy night with humble prayer, but before we pray someone says something about Bobby, about how tomorrow will no doubt be hard. We thank everyone for the ways they've loved us through this pain, for the stories they still tell about Bobby. My Aunt Beth says, "Bobby was a person you don't forget." Smiles spill across every face.

My dad leads the prayer. After an hour of talking through the hardest things our family has ever had to face, Dad prays mostly thanksgiving, ending with these words: "Father, we truly count it all joy to have fallen into troublesome times." He says, "These things drew us closer to You and to one another." He says, "They made us better."

Later, before everyone has left, a cousin will call on the phone, and we'll all sing together. We'll sing "The Joy of the Lord is My Strength."

Has it always been this way? Have we always laughed and prayed and praised in the face of loss? Have we always been united in peace and perspective?

No.

But did this night happen just as I've recorded it?

Yes. Yes it did.

After the party, my mom and I get into an argument. That is exactly the wrong word for it; we're not "opposed," but I can't think of another that captures the tension and temperature. Mostly it's a discussion in which I am chronically misunderstanding her and crying.

I realize, an hour or so in, how much she still misses my brother, how hard it is to live far away from me and her grandkids. Since Bobby died, we've only lived in the same city for two out of fifteen years. I realize how bad it's been to grieve apart. I realize how little time I've spent thinking about my parents' grief. I realize all this tension I'm feeling, this unchecked emotion, is guilt.

This grief has been good in a dozen ways, but it hasn't been all good. Grief has made me selfish.

I go to bed angry.

I wake up to light streaming through the window and my mom's forgiveness.

~

December 13, 2017, is nothing like December 13, 2002. It is a perfect Florida day, sunny and sixty. I wake in the safety of my parents' home. I wake closer to lunch than breakfast. Mom and I meet Dad for lunch. We eat Cuban sandwiches on a patio.

Later, Mom and I drive to the wreck site about an hour away. I haven't been in more than fourteen years. I read to her from this book. She fills in details, corrects things I've misremembered. She tells me Dad didn't go to the wreck site to get Bobby's things. She says the car had been towed to a farm. Dad bagged up Bobby's stuff, with the help of my uncles, in a barn. She said the farmer didn't know what to say.

We're coming up on the place from the opposite direction Bobby would have been coming. Everything in every direction is fields—every view the same view—which makes remembering hard. We drive by the mile marker, and I miss it. We make a U-turn. We get close, and I notice the way the road curves ahead. I remember that. I remember thinking he wouldn't have turned the steering wheel. We pull off and see the "Drive Safely" sign the state has installed in his memory. This doesn't look anything like what I remember.

I remember more space between the tree line and the road. I remember less brush, fewer vines. I don't remember this fence and the field on the other side. But here is the sign with my brother's name printed on it, so we must be close. Mom finds cleaner in the car and takes to the tired sign. I wander, looking for the offending tree, looking for any sign something happened here.

I can't find the tree. I find one that looks like it's been struck by lightning, but it seems too small to stop a car. I find another, wider, but I can't envision a path from the road to this tree. I plot trajectories and measure distances, but nothing makes sense. I get on my hands and knees and dig in the dirt looking for glass or car fragments. Nothing. There is no evidence my brother died here. I write in my notebook, "How dare these trees be so unphased?"

My mom yells over the road noise, "It's been fifteen years. The ground's shifted. That tree might not even be here anymore." She's right. Time changes things.

I give up my efforts to find the tree and instead ask God, "If there's something You want me to see, show me." I think of the last time I was here and finding the plastic turtle.

I look and look and look. I climb over and through vines, pull thorns from my arms and legs. I walk the fence behind the tree line. I want to find something meaningful to bring me comfort. But there's nothing here.

Resolved to leave, I look for my mom and find her standing a hundred feet away, staring at the field just beyond the fence. A shaft of sunlight streams through the canopy of trees above her, alighting on her platinum hair and strong shoulders. And I realize perhaps my mom is what God wants me to see.

I think back to my dream, the one where Bobby told me he'd left me something. Maybe he wasn't talking about a turtle. Maybe he was talking about my parents.

I meet up with Mom at the sign, and I ask if she'll pray before we go. Neither of us is crying. Our hands don't shake. She prays like Dad, her words drenched in thanksgiving. She tells God, "Thank You that he was almost home. And now he is."

But that's not all she prays. She confesses, too. Confesses for both of us. Tells God we're sorry we haven't loved each other as well as we should have.

We ride home in peace. I eat a sugar cookie, the exact kind Bobby and I would get on grocery shopping trips as children. I've bought this cookie for this moment—I eat one and leave one, like you might pour out a shot for an old friend. But I'm hungry, so I eat Bobby's cookie, too. It's in keeping with the character of our relationship.

We pick up Dad and go to the cemetery just as the sun starts to set. The plaza where Bobby is interred is newly littered with statues and plaques, commemorative benches and birdbaths. It looks like a Floridian's front yard. But Bobby's marker is the same. A marble square with the names Peggy S. Martin and Robert D. Mays. A friend of his has left a card. She leaves one every year on this day. She might have been my sister-in-law if he'd lived. He loved her best.

My dad peruses other people's plots; he likes these brass plates with photographs etched onto them. He wonders aloud which photo he'd pick. My mom reads the friend's letter. I sit down on the cement and stare at Robert D. Mays' name, a name he almost never used.

I imagine his body in there, decomposed of course, but also mostly contained inside that box, all the dust that once was him waiting to be reassembled and glorified.

I expected to feel sad. I do a little. I don't a little.

I find myself anticipating the resurrection. I tell Bobby it's coming soon. I make plans for what we'll do when it happens. I dream up a thousand memories we'll make together then. I think about introducing him to my kids—brave London and joyful Eve. I think of him and me and Justin meeting my kids I've never held, the ones I miscarried, and I'm glad he'll be there for the moment. I wonder if he'll have bubblegum cigars.

All of this is coming. All of it is real.

I miss having Bobby here, and that makes me sad. I *do* cry. But I realize I'm not missing much—just a couple or few dozen years. What's that in light of an eternity together? *Mist.*

ecc

The thing people want to know after they've lost a loved one is, "Is it always going to be like this? Am I ever going to feel good again? Will my life ever go back to normal?"

The answer is more complicated than we wish it was. It depends on who you lost and what you lost when you lost them. It depends on who you have around you. It depends on your response to the pain. It depends on whether or not you have hope. It depends on your accountability. It depends on who you listen to. It depends on how willing you are to move forward or how anchored you stay in the past. Sometimes it depends on the weather. Sometimes it depends on how much money you have in your bank account or who you run into at the grocery store or whether or not you're drinking enough water. It mostly depends on resurrection, your faith in it, and your devotion to living it.

Every journey through grief is different. We start and "end" in different places. There are few paved roads or street signs. Grief is a wilderness wandering.

I wrote this book because, for me, fifteen years after losing my brother and best friend, things are better than they were. I found a path that led to light and life. I feel good these days. I play games with my kids. I get out of bed when the alarm goes off. I go on vacation and don't worry we're all going to die in a parasailing accident. I have a beautiful marriage full of freedom and hope. I can sometimes go a whole day without a single melancholy memory. I can see pictures of Bobby or hear stories about Bobby and be genuinely happy, happy I had a brother like him, happy I'll see him again.

I'm not buried anymore. I'm alive.

Death has been swallowed up in victory.

I wrote this book to let you know: You can survive. Resurrection is available on this side of the grave, too.

What I can't promise is total healing. I can't promise you'll ever stop hurting entirely. My husband says healing from grief is like the healing of a massive wound. Over the years the wound shrinks in surface area. You're less likely to bump it against a table or brush your hand against it getting dressed. People poke it less and less often. Soon the wound is barely visible and rarely gets bumped. But when it does get bumped, it hurts. It can hurt as much as it ever has. The wound isn't wide anymore, but it will always be deep.

My parents and I stayed in a hotel room in Orlando on the night of the 13th. We wanted to be close to the airport so I wouldn't miss my early flight the next morning. We picked a fancy hotel, ordered New York-style pizza, and watched TV sitcoms.

When I was a kid, we'd grocery shop on Fridays after Dad got his check. Next to the grocery store was a New York-style pizza place my parents had been ordering from since they were teenagers. Most Fridays, mom would order a pizza on her way out of the store. We'd take it home and eat it together, the four of us, watching TGIF on ABC.

This night felt like those nights did.

Right before bed I jotted some things down, notes on the trip, a prayer of thanksgiving. "Thank You for parents who love me, for transformation through trials, for Your presence and promise…" I scribbled, "We ate pizza and watched TV sitcoms and it felt comfortable and familiar, all four of us packed onto one king-size bed."

I didn't realize until I got home, until this moment as I write this chapter and transcribe my notes, that I'd written "four of us" and not "three.

ABOUT THE AUTHOR

Jennifer (JL) Gerhardt is a writer and storytelling minister. Her previous books include *Prayer, In Practice*, *Think Good: How to get rid of anxiety, guilt, despair, and the like to finally find peace of mind,* and *Live or Die: a study in Philippians.* She blogs at godscout.com. As a storytelling minister for Round Rock Church of Christ, she enables God's people to share their stories of redemption, rescue, and belonging in Christ.

Jennifer is married to Justin Gerhardt, a preacher, and together they have two daughters, London and Eve. Jennifer is an INFJ, lover of chai tea lattes, recreational swimmer, believer in the power of white paint and Dietrich Bonhoeffer fangirl.

To keep up with JL Gerhardt, subscribe to her newsletter at godscout.com/subscribe

www.godscout.com

28125714R00112

Made in the USA
Lexington, KY
14 January 2019